READING WORKOUT

A Program for New Students of English

Jann Huizenga
College of Santa Fe

Maria Thomas-Ružić
University of Colorado

HEINLE & HEINLE PUBLISHERS
A Division of Wadsworth, Inc.
Boston, Massachusetts 02116

The Publication of *Reading Workout* was directed by the members of the
Newbury House Publishing Team at Heinle & Heinle:

Erik Gundersen, Editorial Director
Kristin Thalheimer, Production Editor

Also participating in the publication of this title were:

Publisher: Stanley J. Galek
Editorial Production Manager: Elizabeth Holthaus
Project Manager: Kyrill Schabert, Waterline Books
Assistant Editor: Karen Hazar
Production Assistant: Maryellen Eschmann
Associate Marketing Manager: Donna Hamilton
Manufacturing Coordinator: Mary Beth Lynch
Interior Designer and Compositor: Margaret Saunders, Pre-Press Company, Inc.
Illustrator: Brian Karas
Cover Artist: Brian Karas
Cover Designer: Bortman Design Group

Photography and Reading Credits: See p. 166.

Library of Congress Cataloging-in-Publication Data

Huizenga, Jann.
    Reading Workout / Jann Huizenga, Maria Thomas-Ružić
        p. cm.
    Includes bibliographical references.
    ISBN 0-8384-3980-2
    1. English language—Textbooks for foreign speakers.   2. Readers.
I. Thomas-Ružić, Maria   II. Title.
PE 1128. H7843   1994
428.6'4—dc20

                                                        93-41026
                                                        CIP

Heinle & Heinle Publishers is a division of Wadsworth, Inc.

10 9 8 7 6 5 4 3 2

CONTENTS

Unit 3 Family Ties   49

Unit 4 Born to Shop   75

ACKNOWLEDGMENTS

Many people contributed to this project. We sincerely thank our international students who piloted some of the materials at an early stage, and those who agreed to share their writing here: Qatip Arifi, Lyudmila Berman, Nicolae Coman, Gianpaolo Conti, Graciela Deoberti, Lazar Dimitrijev, Steve Gallegos, Michi Ishida, Rina Martemianova, Quy Thu Nguyen, Nancy Rascon, Biljana Shopova, Dominika Szmerdt and Mako Ushizawa.

We appreciate the input of colleagues and grad students, some of whom helped us articulate our ideas about teaching reading, and others who encouraged us to come up with a reading text to use in conjunction with *Writing Workout.* We're grateful, too, to our reviewers Litza Georghiou of Union County College (NJ), Colleen Weldele of Palomar College (CA), and Nancy Pfingstag of the University of North Carolina, Charlotte. Their comments and criticisms were tremendously helpful throughout the developmental process. Special thanks to Donna Omata at the International English Center, University of Colorado at Boulder, who field-tested parts of *Reading Workout* and gave us valuable feedback.

At Heinle & Heinle, we'd like to thank our editor, Erik Gundersen, for his constant encouragement, gentle manner and big smile. It was a real pleasure to work with him. Production Editor Kristin Thalheimer did a great job coordinating piles of photos, permissions, design and production. Kyrill Schabert was responsible for the nitty-gritty production and we thank him for his wonderful attention to detail and great patience.

Finally, we'd like to thank our families. Kim Crowley's and Ranko Ružić's photos and ideas have inproved this book; their suppport and encouragement helped make it possible. Mia would like to thank Luka Ružić, Lloyd Thomas and Lydia Thomas for the many special ways in which they contributed, and Jann thanks John and Dolly Huizenga for their loving support. The authors are thankful for a long friendship and professional collaboration beginning in Bosnia, and would like to dedicate this book to colleagues, friends and peacemakers there.

ABOUT THIS BOOK

Reading Workout is a self-contained reading text for high beginning English as a Second Language (ESL) or English as a Foreign Language (EFL) students. Its five, content-based units provide enough material for a 35- to 50-hour course, depending on the proficiency of the students, the goals and nature of the course, and other factors. If full use is made of the book's various options and extension activities, *Reading Workout* can provide material for a longer course.

Reading Workout can ideally be used with *Writing Workout,* a high-beginning writing program, and *All Talk* (Heinle and Heinle, 1992), an oral skills program based on problem solving and critical thinking skills development for high beginners. The advantages of using two or more books from this content-based series derive largely from the fact that the unit themes in all three books parallel and complement one another. Each book is organized around the following five themes: 1) Homes, 2) Health, 3) Family Ties, 4) Shopping and Money matters, and 5) Going Places. Whether used on their own, or in conjunction with one another, the books are designed to promote meaningful and integrated language practice around a highly interactive "whole learner" approach.

CONTENT-BASED ORGANIZATION AND APPROACH

The organizing principle of *Reading Workout* is content, rather than language or skills practice. We see motivation as a crucial factor in learning to read in a second language, and by encouraging students to experience reading as a meaning-making process, the text not only fosters literate behaviors appropriate in North American educational and social settings, it keeps students motivated to continue to learn to read in English. As second language reading experts Eskey and Grabe note, "The content and quality of text that second laguage students are asked to read may be the most important determinants of whether, and to what degree, such students do in fact develop (reading) skills (1988)."

The five content-based units in *Reading Workout* have been developed not only to sustain motivation but also to enhance students' comprehension. *In-depth* reading, in which students read several texts on the same topic or theme (there are seven per unit), lightens the cognitive load for readers by providing a predictable framework. That is, new content schemata do not need to be formed each time a new text appears. Rather, students can build on what has come before as they progress through a unit. The content of each reading text, although fresh and engaging, is in most cases also familiar and everyday. All of these contextual supports build in predictability for the reader, and, ultimately, provide for better comprehension.

ACTIVITIES

The number of activities and exercises in *Reading Workout* has been streamlined so as not to overshadow the process of reading itself. The activities included have several aims:

1) **To model good reading strategies** (see **Reading Strategies** below). The tasks students do for each text have real-life relevance; they are set up as models for how a good reader might approach the text.

2) **To foster the kind of literate relationship with texts that needs to be developed in North American academic and social contexts.** Successful readers do much more than retrieve information from a text, and it is this awareness that *Reading Workout* seeks to promote. The tasks encourage interactive reading: comparing what one reads with personal experience, evaluating text, expressing one's opinion, and so on. Activities focusing on locating and retrieving information from a text play just a small part in *Reading Workout* for, as Blanton writes, "always reading for the "right" answer (to someone else's) questions denies students opportunities to understand the transactional nature of the relationship between reader and writer" and renders readers powerless before a text (1992). *Reading Workout* aims rather to develop in students what Blanton calls a "posture of authority" vis a vis a reading text: an awareness that they can and should ask their own questions and state their own opinions and reactions to what they read.

3) **To develop an interactive community of readers.** In real life, we discuss what we read with others, and make what we read an integral part of our social and professional communication. This allows us to clarify our thoughts and encourages us to read further on a topic. *Reading Workout* provides numerous opportunities for this type of interaction, which we see as vital to readers' growth and motivation, particularly at beginning levels in English. Pair, group, and even whole-class sharing, discussion, and jig-saw type activities are interwoven at every stage.

4) **To develop overall language and communication ability.** At every stage, reading is integrated with writing, speaking and listening. Language-focused vocabulary development is interwoven throughout, without intruding or disrupting the flow of activity.

INCLUSION OF AUTHENTIC READING MATERIALS

Most authentic or unsimplified materials have been generally reserved for use with intermediate and advanced level students. However, students at lower levels stand to gain at least as much by exposure to well-selected authentic texts appropriate to their interests and abilities. Thus, *Reading Workout* makes the greatest possible use of authentic and near-authentic texts which have been altered by some omissions and, in some cases, slight rewording. In our experience, authentic texts motivate readers at this level, and authentic presentations of texts provide rich contextual information in the way of photographs, illustrations, captions, headings, subheadings, and quoted materials, which help readers get meaning from the text.

TREATMENT OF VOCABULARY

Reading Workout departs from the assumptions made by traditional reading texts about the way vocabulary should be treated. Often in these texts, vocabulary is highlighted and drilled to such an extent that students come away with the misconception that reading means understanding every word in the text. They lose sight of the forest for the trees, stopping at each new word and failing to read quickly for overall meaning. *Reading Workout* recognizes that students' lack of vocabulary can be compensated for to some extent by the use of good reading strategies, and it aims to have students learn to use these systematically and appropriately. Training students to activate and use their background knowledge, read globally first for general comprehension, ask questions, guess meanings from context, and talk with fellow students are some of the ways that compensatory strategies are encouraged. Thus, **Reading Workout** has made a conscious choice to provide more holistic reading practice for learners by moving the focus *away* from vocabulary- and language-specific exercises and *onto* text- and world-relevant tasks that help students read strategically. (See Reading Strategies below).

Reading Workout does, however, encourage and promote vocabulary acquisition in second language reading. Students are trained to develop and organize their own Word Banks. We feel that student-generated vocabulary entries have the advantage of allowing students to capture those words that are, in the words of Carroll and Mordaunt, on their "frontier or verge of mastery." (1991) Making students responsible for vocabulary in this way also trains them to become self-sufficient learners. In addition to the Word Bank, students have ample opportunity to work on their own or with others on vocabulary development exercises in the Vocabulary Appendix.

SYSTEMATIC TRAINING IN THE DEVELOPMENT OF READING STRATEGIES

Reading Workout does, however, encourage and promote vocabulary acquisition in second language reading. Students are trained to develop and organize their own Word Banks. We feel that student-generated vocabulary entries have the advantage of allowing students to capture those words that are, in the words of Carroll and Mordaunt, on their "frontier or verge of mastery (1991)." Making students responsible for vocabulary in this way also trains them to become self-sufficient learners. In addition to the Word Bank, students have ample opportunity to work on their own or with others on vocabulary development exercises in the Vocabulary Appendix.

Thus, the strategy training, together with the content focus of **Reading Workout** helps students develop strategic literacy behaviors that contribute to successful second language reading. Students' reading and thinking processes can be centered on general meaning and strategies for meeting task demands, rather than on reading skills concepts, such as "find the main idea" or "check your comprehension." Strategic reading, then, views reading as a whole, rather than a compilation of isolated skills and exercises. Ultimately, we see that the introduction of basic reading strategies can help promote greater reader independence.

FLEXIBILITY

There are a number of ways in which this book offers flexibility and options to both students and instructors. First, not all texts in each unit have to be read. A class can decide at the outset of each unit what to cover and what to skip. This can be done right after Reading 1 of each unit, which functions as an overview "quiz" for the unit. Second, the text offers students opportunities to do extra work on their own: the Vocabulary Appendix features self-study vocabulary development exercises and the Optional Reading 7 in each unit gives motivated students something extra to read. Third, students have options and control in developing their Word Banks. Finally, the Instructor's Notes offer flexibility and additional ideas for teachers.

REFERENCES

Blanton, L. L. 1992. Reading, writing and authenticity issues in developmental ESL. In *College ESL* 2 (1).

Carrell, P. L. 1989. Metacognitive awareness and second language reading. *Modern Language Journal* (3), 121-134.

Carroll, M. C. and Morduant, O.G. 1991. The frontier method of vocabulary practice. In *TESOL Journal,* Autumn 1991.

Eskey, D. E. and Grabe, W. 1988. Interactive models for second language reading: perspectives on instruction. In Carrell, et al. (eds), *Interactive Approaches to Second Language Reading,* Cambridge: Cambridge University Press.

1

Home, Sweet Home

WARMING UP: *Talking About Homes*

1–A Work with a partner. Ask these questions:

Do you live in an apartment, dorm, or house?

Do you like your home? (In the U.S.? In your country?) Why or why not?

Is there something unusual or special about your home?

1–B Write down any words or phrases that you associate with the idea of "home."

_____

_____

_____

_____

_____

_____

Share some of your words with the class.

1–C Which of these words do you associate with your home or homes in general? Circle them. Then tell why.

family   music   door   luck

yard   walls   happy

furniture   architect

aluminum cans   windows

quiet   money   bed   street

READING 1: *Quiz on Homes*

1–D   How much do you know about homes? With a partner, circle the best answer.

Quiz on Homes

1. In which country do people usually keep doors to their rooms and offices open?
    a)   Germany   b)   Korea
    c)   the U.S.   d)   all of these

2. What do people in Japan use a *futon* for?
    a)   eating   b)   helping a headache
    c)   sleeping   d)   drawing

3. In which culture is it lucky for the owner's bedroom to be in the southwest corner of the house?
    a)   Chinese   b)   Italian
    c)   Nigerian   d)   all of these

4. Some materials that can be used to build a house are wood, stone, and . . .
    a)   car tires   b)   cans
    c)   bricks   d)   all of these

5. About how many children in the world live and support themselves on city streets?
    a)   25 million   b)   100 million
    c)   250 million d)   1 billion

1–E   Now look at the next page and check your answers.

How many did you get correct? _____

READING 1

Answers to quiz

1. *c)*   In offices and homes in the United States, doors tend to stay open. Of course, sometimes Americans close doors, too. See Reading 2 for more facts about the inside of homes around the world.

2. *c)*   In Japan, many people use a *futon* for sleeping—not a bed. In Reading 3, learn more about homes in Japan and in Russia.

3. *a)*   Many Chinese believe that there are lucky and unlucky things about a house. These ideas come from *feng shui.* See Reading 4.

4. *d)*   Old used car tires and aluminum cans don't need to go into the garbage! Reading 5 tells about an unusual house in New Mexico that is made of these waste materials.

5. *b)*   There are about 100 million homeless children in the world, and about one-third of these children live in Brazil. See the article about Alexandro in Reading 6.

READING 2: *Inside Homes Around the World*

 1–F   Talk with a partner about this house. Does it look like houses in your country? Why or why not? Would you like to live here?

Write some words or phrases to describe it.

_____

_____

_____

_____

READING 2

1–G Look over the reading text on these pages. Name two things a good reader might do <u>before</u> reading the text. Then look at the Reading Strategy box.

Do you know much about this topic? Read to see if you learn anything new. Put a check (✓) in the margin next to the things *you already know* and a cross mark (✗) next to information that is new.

READING STRATEGIES

1. **Before you read, get the general idea by looking at the title and subheadings. You can also read the first paragraph. This is called** *previewing* **a text.**

2. **Always try to connect the things you already know with the things you are reading.**

Inside Homes Around the World

1   Walk inside a home in a new country, and it can look and feel so different! One big difference is the organization of the inside, or interior space. For example, rooms in a house are *usually* separated by walls—but *not always,* and not in the same
5   ways.

The use of walls and doors

In many parts of the Arab world, people like to have homes with very large spaces, and they avoid **partitions.** Anthropologist Edward Hall explains that Arabs like to be
10   together, so they don't look for privacy in separate spaces in the home.

Hall claims that Germans, on the other hand, like privacy. They have thick walls and heavy doors in their homes. And these doors are often closed. But in the U.S., doors in the house
15   (and at the office, too) usually stay open. When a door is closed, it is probably for a private conversation, or for study, resting, sleeping, dressing, or sex.

Some modern homes in the U.S. and other places have no walls at all. This arrangement is an "open floor plan."

20   **A special kind of wall**

The walls in traditional Japanese and Korean homes are **unique.** They are **semi-fixed** walls, or partitions. These are made of light wooden frames covered with special paper. The partitions are movable, so that rooms can be used for different
25   purposes, such as sleeping, talking, or studying.

Furniture

Another big difference among homes is in the type of furniture, and where it is placed in the room. Homes in the U.S. look **cluttered** to many visitors because they are full of chairs, tables

1–H   Did you learn anything new? Tell a partner.

1–I   Read the text a second time. As you read, try to fill in the boxes with a word or two. This helps you remember the information.

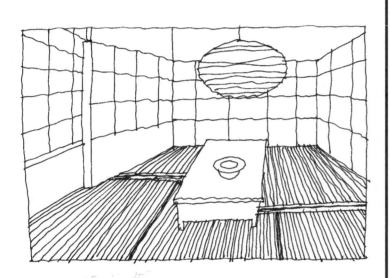

	Japan	Germany	The U.S.
doors	*X*	*heavy, often closed.*	
walls			
furniture			

30   and chests. Americans often place the furniture around the walls. In Japan, however, furniture is often in the center of the room, and sometimes there is *no* furniture. In German homes the furniture is traditionally solid and heavy, and it stays fixed in one place. In many
35   countries, including Ethiopia and Iran, Japan, Laos and Turkey, to name only a few, people often prefer to sit on floor mats or beautiful rugs, and *not* on chairs. Thus, rooms can have less furniture than in the West.

Closed doors, open doors, or no doors; thick walls,
40   paper walls, no walls; lots of furniture, little furniture, or no furniture at all—these are just some of the differences we find from home to home, place to place.

*

partition	a divider or wall
unique	special, one-of-a-kind
semi-fixed	partly attached
cluttered	crowded

READING 3: *Homes in My Country*

1–J We asked two international students to write about homes in their countries. Choose *just one* description to read now.

As you read, decide what you like best about either Japanese homes or Russian homes.

Mako Ushizawa is a student from Japan. She describes things you can find in a typical home in Japan.

A single-family house in Japan has one or more tatami-mat rooms. A tatami mat is a rug made of straw. The tatami-mat room has paper sliding doors which are called "shoji" in Japanese. The shoji is made of wooden frames and white Japanese paper. Shoji are used instead of curtains.

In Japan, some people use beds for sleeping, but many people use a futon instead. We take the futon out of the closet at night and in the morning we roll up the futon and put it away in the closet. Our closet door is called a "fusama." It is a wooden frame covered with pictures on Japanese paper.

This is Lyudmila Berman. She compares and contrasts homes in her native Russia with homes in the U.S.

The architecture of houses in Russia is different than in the U.S. Buildings in modern towns in Russia are usually tall (five stories or more). Here in the USA, they are not tall; even a three-story building is not common (except in big cities).

All the rooms in Russian apartments have walls and doors. Here, some rooms are not separated from each other. For example, in my apartment, the kitchen, dining room, and living room are one big open space.

In Russia, the walls are usually covered with wallpaper, which is often very beautiful. Here, I have only seen wallpaper in kitchens. Our floors are usually wood. There is no wall-to-wall carpeting. But often we have very nice rugs on the floor.

Houses in villages and some towns in Russia don't have modern conveniences such as toilets, bathrooms, and cold and hot water inside the house. Toilets are outside the house, and water has to be taken from wells.

Houses here are big, comfortable, and well equipped, but in Russia they are cozier.

Find one or two classmates who read the description that *you did not read.* Tell each other about what you read. Then describe houses in your country.

1-K   Write in a journal about homes in your country, or about your own home.

READING 4: *Lucky Houses*

1–L   In North America, the following things are considered lucky or unlucky by some people.

Lucky Things

Unlucky Things

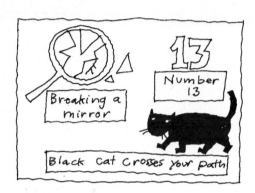

What things do people in your country consider lucky or unlucky? Make a list with the class.

1–M   Preview Reading 4. Look at the title, pictures, and captions. Do you think a house can be lucky (or unlucky)? Read and decide what you think about the Asian view of "lucky" houses. Write your opinion.

> **READING STRATEGY**
>
> In North America, students are often asked to give a personal opinion about what they read. Is this the same in your country?

If you have classmates from Asia, think of a question to ask them about the idea of "luck."

Question:

READING 4

Lucky Houses

People in California are learning about the Chinese art of feng shui.

By Philip Langdon

1 Michael Ho is a seventy-two-year-old retired professor from Hong Kong. He is a lean man with gray hair, and he owns a
5 home in Covina Palms, an area outside Los Angeles.

Before Ho bought his house in Covina Palms, he had looked at a house in an area
10 called Hillcrest. Ho didn't buy the Hillcrest house, because it had several major problems. It was *unlucky,* according to Ho.

"The front and **rear** doors
15 were in a straight line, without any **obstruction,**" said Ho.

The Hillcrest house had another problem in the main bedroom, Ho recalled: "It was
20 difficult to find a **suitable** place to put the bed."

Why were these things problems?

Ho and many Asians
25 believe that some houses are "lucky" or "unlucky" because of *feng shui* (pronounced fung-shway). *Feng shui* is the Chinese word for "the art of
30 placement." *Feng shui* tries to create a good relationship between people and all the things around them.

For example, according to
35 *feng shui,* a straight path from the front to the rear door allows **cosmic** energy (*ch'i*) to come in and out of the house too fast. This may mean that
40 the money, peace, and happiness of the people who live in the house can escape too easily. This was a problem in the Hillcrest house.

45 *Feng shui* dictates that the owner's bedroom should be in a particular part of the house—usually in the house's southwest corner. And some
50 Chinese think it is very bad when the foot of the bed faces the door, because this echoes the Chinese way of positioning dead people with feet toward
55 the door. In the Hillcrest house, it was hard to find a good or "lucky" position for the bed.

There are many Asians in
60 California who want to buy "lucky" houses, so building companies are listening to Michael Ho. They want to know more about *feng shui.*
65 What about you?

This is an adaptation of an article by the same title that first appeared in **The Atlantic Monthly,** *November 1991. The illustration by artist Mike Quon also accompanied the original article.*

---

*
rear	back
obstruction	something that blocks the way
suitable	fitting, right
cosmic	from the universe

READING 4

1–N   Read "Lucky Houses" a second time.

With a partner, decide which one of these three floor plans is lucky for Professor Ho. <u>Underline</u> the parts of the text that support your choice.

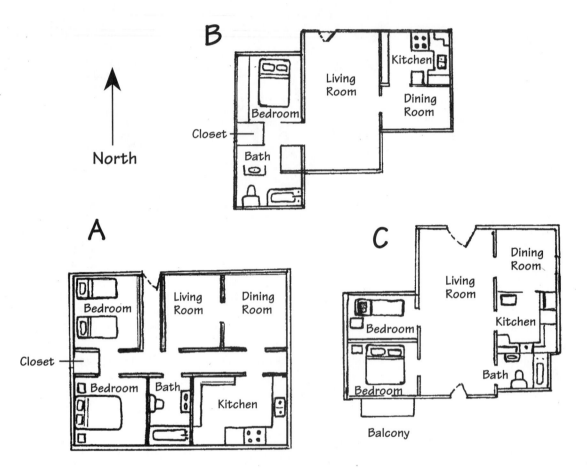

Check your answer with the class.

1–O   What new words do you want to remember from the text? Circle them and then write them in your Word Bank (see p. 143).

1–P   **Independent Vocabulary Study:** Description Words. Turn to page 122 in the Vocabulary Appendix.

READING 5: *Tires Are Hub of New Walls*

1–Q   The newspaper article in Reading 5 is about an unusual kind of house called an "earthship." Preview the article.

With the class, write questions that you have about this house.

> **READING STRATEGY**
>
> Asking yourself questions before reading can help you concentrate and comprehend.

Question:

Question:

Question:

Question:

1–R   Read to find the answers. <u>Underline</u> them in the text.

With the class, discuss the answers you found.

READING 5

TIRES ARE HUB OF NEW WALLS

"Best kind of house"

By Kay Bird

1   It's an **environmentalist's** dream: a home that uses lots of **waste** materials.

    The environmentalist's
5   dream is Janet Degan's and Craig Siegel's reality: a large home in Santa Fe, New Mexico, built from used tires, aluminum cans and
10 dirt.

    "I love it," said Degan recently during a break from the construction work. "I'm a **landscape** architect and I
15 think this is the best kind of house you can have."

    The homes—there are 80 of them in New Mexico and Colorado—are called earth-
20 ships. They are the creation of architect Michael Reynolds, who started designing houses out of **recycled** tires and cans in
25 the 1970s.

    Degan and Siegel esti-mate that 800 tires will be used to make the walls. Each tire is packed with dirt.

* environmentalist
   a person who wants to protect nature
waste
   things that are thrown away, garbage
landscape
   the area around buildings, or open spaces
recycled
   used again.
square foot
   1'x1', or 144 square inches (about 930 cm²)
benefits
   help, advantages
upper body workout
   exercise for the arms and chest

1–S Read the article again and fill in the chart box.

30 The thick walls will <u>absorb</u> heat during the day and release it at night. The combination of elements will keep the <u>interior</u> tempera-
35 ture at about 60° F (15° C).

The materials for the Degan–Siegal house are much less expensive than for normal houses. Old tires
40 are often given away by tire stores. And Degan picks up cans while she jogs. "One time I got six bags," she said. The total cost will be
45 about $50 per **square foot,** or $75,000.

Building the house also has health **benefits.** "It's like a free gym," she said.
50 "It's a great **upper body workout.** It's the funnest thing I've ever done."

From **The New Mexican,** *May 17, 1992 (adapted)*

Type of house: _earth–ship_

Owners: _Janet Degan and Craig Siegel's_

Architect: _Michael Reynolds_

Location (state): _____

Materials: _____

Cost: _____

Would you like to live in the Degan–Siegel home? Tell a partner why or why not.

The Degan-Siegel house under construction.

1–T **Independent Vocabulary Study:** Modifiers and Nouns. Turn to page 123 in the Vocabulary Appendix.

READING 6: *Brazil's Children of the Streets*

1–U   What do you know or think about homeless people in North America or other parts of the world? Tell the class.

Preview Reading 6. Who are the "children of the streets"? What are they doing in the picture?

1–V   Read the article quickly to check your ideas. Then tell a partner what you understood.

1–W   Reread the article. Fill in the chart as you read. It will help you to *summarize* the important information.

READING STRATEGY

We often need to give only main, important ideas from an original story. When we do this, we *summarize* the story. Summarizing is an important reading strategy for readers to practice.

Summary Chart: Brazil's Children of the Streets

WHO is the article about?

_____

WHAT's the problem?

_____

WHERE does the story happen?

_____

WHY?

_____

WHEN does it happen?

_____

HOW MANY people are in this situation?

_____

Work with a partner. Compare your charts.

1–X   Write in your journal about Alexandro or about the problem of homelessness in general. Does the problem exist in your country? What can we do about it?

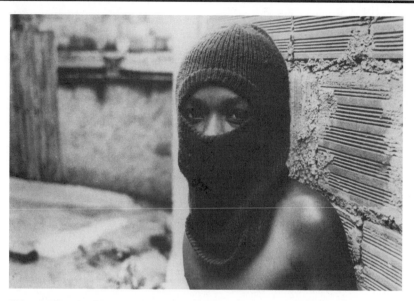

This young boy, hooded to hide his identity, works as a drug runner, lookout and messenger for cocaine traffickers at a Rio shantytown.

Brazil's
CHILDREN
OF THE STREETS

■ *While as many as 100 million children support themselves on city streets throughout the world, almost a third of them live in Brazil.*

By Michaela Jarvis

1 At 5 or 6 years old, they sell candy or shine shoes, **beg** or steal. The children deliver drugs for traffickers, or they **prostitute.** They look for food in trash cans. They sniff **glue.** Many can-
5 not spell their own first names, and they will never **set foot in** a classroom.

They are street children, and today you can find them everywhere in the Brazilian seaport of Rio de Janeiro.

10 Alexandro is a street child in Rio. He is 11 years old. For more than five years he has been living in the streets, sleeping in a downtown **plaza** on a bed of cardboard and newspapers. He wears a dirty, dusty T-shirt, shorts, and no
15 shoes.

He is small for his age, with short, curly brown hair. He has the eyes of an old man. His mother lives about an hour away by bus, in a housing project outside of the city. His stepfa-
20 ther won't let him stay there, because the family is poor. Sometimes Alexandro goes to visit his mother and takes her the money he gets from begging or stealing.

"I wish I had a beautiful house," Alexandro
25 says. "I wish I could play soccer and joke and have some clothes."

All of us, no doubt, wish the same thing for Alexandro.

From **St. Petersburg Times,** *May 19, 1991 (adapted)*

---

beg	ask for (without paying)
prostitute	offer sex for money
glue	thick substance for sticking things together
set foot in	walk into
plaza	city or town square

READING 6

1–Y When we summarize, we tell only the main ideas of the original text. One difficult part about writing a summary is in the reading. Sometimes it is hard to see the difference between a main idea and a detail. Summarizing is an important skill in university work.

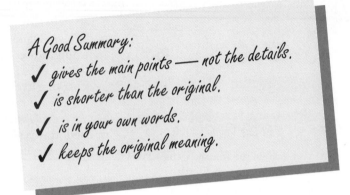

A Good Summary:
- ✓ *gives the main points — not the details.*
- ✓ *is shorter than the original.*
- ✓ *is in your own words.*
- ✓ *keeps the original meaning.*

Look at the three summaries of "Brazil's Children of the Streets" below. Only one is a good summary. Try to find it.

A

> I like Alexandro. He is a small boy with curly hair. He sleeps in downtown Rio de Janeiro in Brazil. He is homeless because he has no parents. We should help him.

B

> Alexandro is a young homeless boy in Rio de Janeiro. He and millions of other children live on the city streets in Brazil. One reason is that their families are poor, writes Michaela Jarvis.

C

> They are street children, and today you can find them everywhere in the Brazilian city of Rio de Janeiro. Alexandro is a street child in Rio. He wishes he had a beautiful house.

What makes one summary better than the others? Discuss this question with the class.

1–Z **Independent Vocabulary Study:** Verbs. Turn to page 124 in the Vocabulary Appendix.

OPTIONAL READING 7

Read another story on a home-related topic if you wish.

In this story, Colette H. Russell describes her life in a shelter for homeless women.

A Day in the Homeless Life

1 *Editor's note: Eighteen months after writing this article, Colette H. Russell was back living in the streets. Nine months later she died alone in a motel room in Las Vegas.*

5 "Good morning, ladies. It's 5 a.m. Time to get up." Ceiling lights were suddenly ablaze. This message boomed repeatedly until nearly everyone was out of bed.

Two toilets and three sinks for 50 10 women; no toilet paper in the morning, **invariably**. Three tables with benches bordered by beds on two sides were our day room, dining room, and lounge.

Breakfast usually arrived at 5:45 15 a.m., too late for those who were in the day-labor **van pools.** They went to work on empty stomachs, and they were the ones needing food the most.

Breakfast generally consisted of 20 rolls and sausage and juice until it ran out. The coffee was unique: It didn't taste like coffee, but that's what we had to drink.

At 6:30 a.m. we were ordered to go 25 down to the lobby, where we joined 50 other women either standing or sitting on wooden benches awaiting the light of day. Some talked to themselves. Some shouted angrily. Some sat motionless.

30 Some slept sitting up. Some jumped up and down, walking away and then returning. Some chain-smoked.

All of us had our belongings with us. Carrying everything every step of the 35 way was hard on the arms.

At 7:30 a.m. the clothing room opened. It was shocking to be told, "Throw away what you're wearing after you get a new outfit." No laundry, just 40 toss out yesterday's garments. We were allotted five minutes to paw through racks looking for articles that fit.

I was always happy to see 8:30 a.m. roll around. Grabbing my bags, I 45 headed down Berkeley Street away from the jam-packed, smoke-filled "holding cell." Always I **felt guilty at** not going to work like everyone else who hurried by as I approached the business district.

50 The main library was my daily stop. I positioned myself at a table where I could watch the clock: We had to return to the shelter before 4 p.m. to get in line for a bed, otherwise we might miss out.

55 Reading was the **high point** of the day. Escape into a book. There was relative privacy at a library table. It was heavenly. I hated to leave.

*Excerpted from **the UTNE Reader,** Sept/Oct 1990.*

---

*	
invariably	(almost) always
van pools	transportation by vans (passenger vehicles)
felt guilty at	felt wrong or bad about
high point	best part

UNIT REVIEW: *Talk It Over*

Walk around your classroom and ask your classmates questions such as:

> *Do you live in an apartment?*
>
> *Do you have an open floor plan?*

Try to write a different name in each blank.

Find someone who

lives in an apartment.   _____

likes an open floor plan.   _____

wants a tire and can house.   _____

believes in good luck.   _____

prefers to sit on the floor.   _____

has a bed facing the door.   _____

knows a homeless person.   _____

likes a lot of privacy.   _____

knows a child who works.   _____

knows what a futon is.   _____

has an environmental home.   _____

has a room with wallpaper.   _____

(Your class can add one.)   _____

UNIT REVIEW: *Writing*

 Write an alphabet poem! Use any words from this unit, and other words you like. Be creative.

Here is one idea for you to get started.

ALL-ABOUT-HOMES ALPHABET POEM

a   apartment, aluminum cans, and Alexandro

b   bed, back doors, books

c   children, cosmic cans, and closed doors

d   dirty T-shirts, drugs and dreams

e   ...

wxyz

Make a bulletin board or poster with everyone's poems. Your teacher may help you to publish them in a booklet.

UNIT REVIEW: *Information Tree*

Bring this information tree to life! Add some leaves that tell what you remember from this unit.

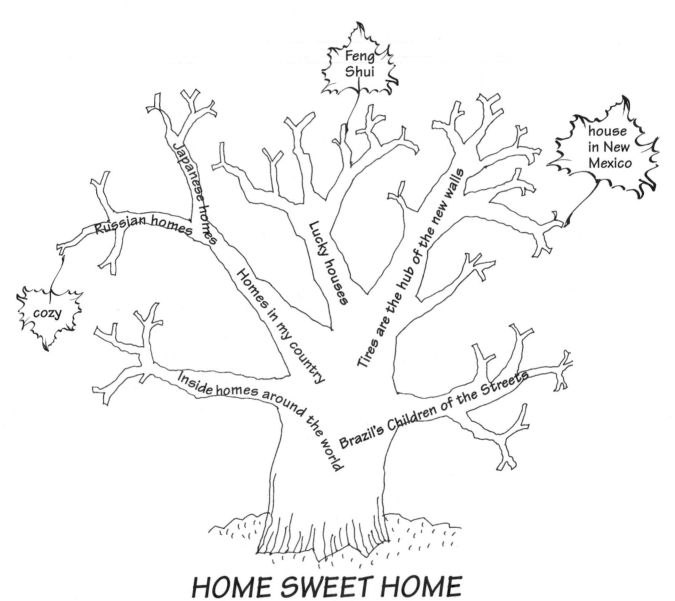

Feng Shui

house in New Mexico

Japanese homes

Russian homes

Lucky houses

Tires are the hub of the new walls

cozy

Homes in my country

Inside homes around the world

Brazil's Children of the Streets

HOME SWEET HOME

 Now compare your tree with a partner's.

UNIT REVIEW: *Word Power*

Fill in the crossword puzzle. The words all appeared in this unit.

Across

2. Where Alexandro sleeps
6. Room for sleeping
7. Chairs, chests and tables are _____.
9. a partition
10. Street children beg or _____ for money.
12. Asian country
13. We throw away _____ materials
15. Alexandro's country
17. An aluminum _____
18. Some people "sniff" this sticky stuff

Down

1. Not rich
3. A round tube for bicycle or car wheels
4. Having no home
5. Something to put on the floor
6. Good, better, the _____
7. The rear door and the _____ door
8. The inside of a building
11. Use aluminum or glass again.
14. In parts of the _____ world, people don't look for privacy.
16. Houses are unlucky or _____ .

Check your answers in the Answer Appendix on page 140.

2

2

To Your Health

WARMING UP: *Talking about health*

2–A   Work with a partner. Ask these questions:

Do you have a healthy diet? Why or why not?

Do you exercise?

Do you smoke?

2–B   Write down any words or phrases that you associate with "good health" and "bad health."

Good Health

_____

_____

_____

Bad Health

_____

_____

_____

Share your ideas with the class.

2–C   Which of these things are especially important for your own personal health? Tell why.

sun   trees   **books**   animals   letters

laughter   dancing   telephone

music   fruit

rain   rice

family   **swimming**   sports

friends   crying   walking

READING 1: *Health Quiz*

2–D   How much do you know about health? With a partner, decide if these sentences are true or false.

Health Quiz

T (F) 1. For a healthy diet, an adult should eat plenty of meat and drink whole milk.

T (F) 2. Running is much better for you than walking.

(T) F 3. Women generally live longer than men.

(T) F 4. Drinking a lot of coffee is not good for you.

T (F) 5. North Americans have one of the healthiest diets in the world.

(T) F 6. Spending too much time alone is unhealthy.

2–E   Now look at the next page and check your answers.

How many did you get correct? _____

READING 1

Answers to health quiz

1. *False.* Both of these foods are high in saturated fat. Saturated fat increases **cholesterol** levels in your blood, which leads to heart disease. Eat meat in small portions only, and drink **skim milk.** See Reading 4 for more information on animal products and heart disease.

2. *False.* Walking can be as good for your heart as running if you walk quickly and often. Also, walking does not **damage** your legs and feet the way running can. See Reading 3 for more information.

3. *True.* Worldwide, women live longer than men. Read more about this in Reading 6.

4. *True.* Too much coffee drinking is unhealthy for several reasons. For details, see Reading 2.

5. *False.* The typical North American diet, high in animal fat and low in vegetables, has been linked to high rates of heart disease and cancer. Read more about this in Reading 4.

6. *True.* Studies have shown that social **isolation** can be a contributing factor in illnesses such as cancer. For further information, see Optional Reading 7.

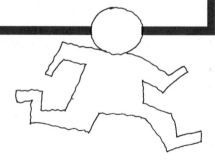

*
cholesterol	a fatty substance in animal fats, blood, and tissue
skim milk	milk with the cream removed
damage	injure, hurt
isolation	separation from other people

READING 2: *Bad Habits*

2–F   What good, healthy habits do you have? Check (✓) the sentences that are true for you and add three others.

_____ I exercise regularly.

_____ I walk to school (or work).

_____ I like to eat fruit.

_____

_____

_____

What bad, unhealthy habits do you have? Check the sentences that are true for you and add three others.

_____ I eat too much.

_____ I don't sleep enough.

_____ I worry too much.

_____

_____

_____

 Now talk about your habits with a partner. Do you share some of the same ones?

READING 2

2-G Look quickly at the magazine article below. How many bad habits does it discuss? ___5___

Put a check (✓) next to the bad habits *you* have. Now read those paragraphs and learn how to break your bad habits.

Bad Habits That Can Ruin Your Health

You know those annoying habits Mother tried to get you to stop? Here's advice on how to break them.

By Wendy Korn

1 **Excessive coffee drinking**
   Side effects. Both regular and decaf-feinated coffee stain teeth and cause stomach irritation. Regular coffee can also contribute
5 to tension and anxiety.
   Habit-breaker. Limit yourself to three cups of coffee a day. Brush your teeth after drinking coffee, and see your dentist for regular professional cleanings.

10 **Grinding teeth in sleep**
   Side effect. It wears down teeth and can eventually loosen them. It can lead to head, back, ear and jaw pain.
15 *Habit-breaker.* See your dentist, who might recommend a night brace or another solution.

Nail biting
   Side effect. In addition to wearing down
20 teeth, chewing nails allows germs in the mouth to transfer to broken skin (and vice versa). It can cause infections under the nail as well as distorted nail growth.
   Habit-breaker. Keep nails well groomed so
25 there are no jagged edges. (Have a nail clipper and nail file handy at all times.) Try wearing Band-Aids over the nails and painting them with bad-tasting iodine.

Salting food before tasting
30 *Side effects.* Too much salt leads to water retention, which is harmful to those with a predisposition to kidney problems, heart disease or high blood pressure.
   Habit-breaker. Remember, the body needs
35 only a small amount of salt per day. Don't leave the salt shaker on the table during meals. Use extra herbs and spices in cooking to bring out full flavor.

Skipping breakfast
40 *Side effects.* The stomach produces acids during the night; without food in the morning, these acids will irritate the stomach. Also, a morning meal provides energy. Without breakfast, you are more likely to suffer from
45 fatigue, an upset stomach, or a headache.
   Habit-breaker. Eat breakfast soon after you awaken. A big meal is not necessary; high-fiber cereal, skim milk and fruit will provide all the energy and nutrition you need,
50 without adding extra calories.

From **Ladies' Home Journal,** *1987 (adapted)*

Then tell a partner which of these bad habits you have and what you just learned about them.

READING 2

2–H   "Bad Habits That Can Ruin Your Health" was organized under five main sub-headings. Can you remember what these main ideas were? Match the left and right columns without looking back.

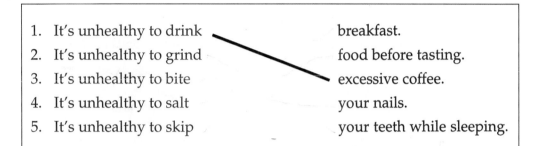

1. It's unhealthy to drink   breakfast.
2. It's unhealthy to grind   food before tasting.
3. It's unhealthy to bite   excessive coffee.
4. It's unhealthy to salt   your nails.
5. It's unhealthy to skip   your teeth while sleeping.

2–I   Look again at the sections you read from "Bad Habits." As you reread, circle the words that are new to you. Can you understand some of them from the context? Use your dictionary only for those words that seem important to the meaning of the text and that you cannot understand from the context.

Choose some new words for your Word Bank.

READING 3: *Exercise Recommendations*

2–J Read about the exercise that the American Health Foundation recommends for a healthy heart. Do you get the recommended amount of aerobic activity?

Yes   No

EXERCISE RECOMMENDATIONS FOR CARDIOVASCULAR FITNESS

The American Health Foundation strongly recommends regular exercise to help maintain good health.

Regular aerobic exercise strengthens the heart and blood vessels, lowers high blood pressure, helps regulate high blood sugar and tones the body while keeping body fat down. Aerobic activity uses large muscle groups, such as the legs, in a rhythmic activity. It can keep you fit when performed for at least thirty minutes three times a week. Brisk walking is the ideal aerobic exercise. It requires no equipment and anyone can do it.

If you are healthy but not active, do not overdo it. Check with your doctor before starting an exercise program, especially if you are 35 or older or may be at special risk for heart disease.

The chart below gives an estimate of the calories that are burned by an average 150-lb person exercising for one hour.

AEROBIC ACTIVITIES	Calories burned/hour	AEROBIC ACTIVITIES	Calories burned/hour
Basketball	360-660	Bicycling	240-420
Bicycling (uphill)	500	Cross-country skiing	600
Dancing	240-420	Running	250-420
Running (11 min. mile)	540	Skating	350-400
Squash/Handball	600	Swimming	540-660
Tennis (singles)	420	Walking (3 mph)	210

Calculate about how many calories you burn in these activities per week. _____

Tell a partner about your weekly activities.

This information was published in a booklet called *Health Passport*. Order it free from American Health Foundation, 1 Dana Rd., Valhalla, NY 10595.

HEALTH PASSPORT

AMERICAN HEALTH FOUNDATION

READING 4: *In Eating Habits, East is Better than West*

2–K Describe your diet. First, fill out the left side of the chart. Then talk to a partner and fill out the right side.

I eat	My partner eats
_____ lots of meat	_____ lots of meat.
_____ lots of pasta, cereal, or bread with whole grains.	_____ lots of pasta, cereal, or bread with whole grains.
_____ fruit everyday.	_____ fruit everyday.
_____ lots of sweets.	_____ lots of sweets.
_____ lots of vegetables.	_____ lots of vegetables.
_____ lots of whole milk, butter, and <u>ice cream</u>.	_____ lots of whole milk, butter, and ice cream.
_____ (other) _____	_____ (other) _____
_____ (other) _____	_____ (other) _____

How can you and your partner improve your diets? Refer to the information below if you wish.

Foods to Eat

Lots of starch and fiber:
Bread, pasta, rice, fruit, beans, vegetables. They're low-fat and low-calorie.

Fish and chicken:
Skinless is better. Bake or broil. Don't fry.

Lean beef, pork and lamb:
Trim off fat. Keep portions small.

Low-fat dairy:
Skim milk, low-fat soft cheese, fat-free yogurt.

Unsaturated vegetable oil:
Corn, canola, safflower, olive, soybean, sesame and sunflower. Tub margarine.

Foods To Avoid

Fatty Meat:
Bacon, bologna, hot dogs and other processed meat, prime beef, cuts rimmed with fat.

High-fat dairy:
Whole milk, hard cheese such as cheddar and Swiss, butter, ice cream.

Saturated oils:
Lard, coconut oil, palm oil.

Sweets:
Doughnuts, Danish, most cookies, cakes, pies and other baked desserts.

Egg yolks:
Substitute whites for whole eggs.

READING 4

2–L   Read the first paragraph of this text. Write one question you have. Then read to find the answer. (Don't stop at new words as you read. Continue, and try to understand them from the context.)

Question:

Answer:

In Eating Habits, East is Better than West

1   Do you want to be healthier and live longer? Then take some lessons from the Chinese. And stay away from the typical North American diet.
   The Chinese eat a healthy, plant-based diet. A joint study by Chinese, American, and British scientists found that although the Chinese diet varies
5   from region to region, it generally includes a lot of rice, grains, and fruit. Animal products are eaten sparingly. In southern China, for instance, almost every meal includes a big bowl of rice. People usually eat a vegetable with the meal, perhaps some fruit, and maybe some fish. Pork and chicken are eaten only on special occasions.
10   The rate for heart disease among men in China is one-sixteenth the rate in the U.S. The rate for colon cancer is only about two-fifths of the U.S. rate. Scientists believe that the poor diet of North Americans is killing them. The average citizen consumes too much meat, sugar and salt and not enough vegetables, grains, and fiber. And these unhealthy eating habits are prime sus-
15   pects in several serious diseases: heart disease, stroke, diabetes, and some cancers.
   T. Colin Campbell, a co-author of the study mentioned above, calls these diseases "diseases of wealth." As countries
20   become richer, people begin to eat more meat. Heart disease and certain kinds of cancer increase. This is happening in Japan, where the traditional low-meat diet is giving way to increased meat
25   consumption. Unfortunately, this is beginning to happen in the wealthier parts of China too. In this case, at least, traditions should be kept.

Is your diet more like the Chinese diet or the North American diet?

READING 4

2–M   Could you understand some of the new words from the context? Look back at the text and see if you can figure out the meanings of these words.

1. joint (line 3)
   a. expensive
   b. shared by two or more people
   c. small

2. varies (line 4)
   a. changes
   b. gets better
   c. increases

3. sparingly (line 6)
   a. by everyone
   b. in small amounts
   c. once a day

4. consumes (line 13)
   a. eats
   b. produces
   c. cooks

5. are prime suspects in (lines 14–15)
   a. are not related to
   b. are caused by
   c. are thought to play a big part in

6. wealth (line 18)
   a. richness
   b. overeating
   c. poverty

READING STRATEGY

Good readers don't stop when they see a new word. They continue reading and try to understand it from the context. Stopping to look up words can result in your losing the main idea of the text.

In a group, talk about why you chose the meaning you did.

READING 4

2–N   Work with a partner. Practice making true sentences using the words in the boxes. Can you each make 3 sentences? Note that this is a *speaking* activity.

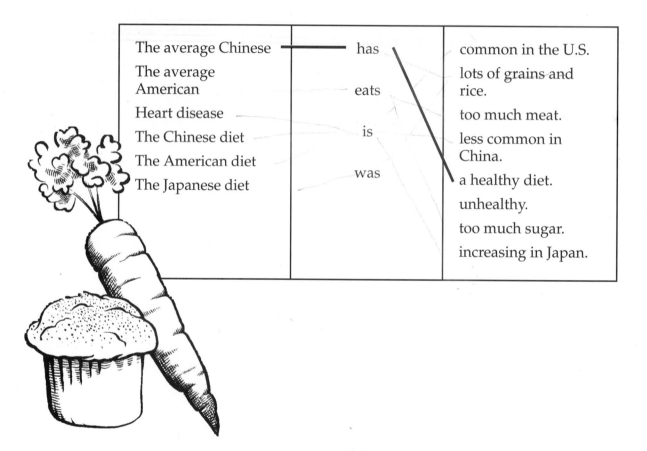

The average Chinese	has	common in the U.S.
The average American	eats	lots of grains and rice.
Heart disease	is	too much meat.
The Chinese diet	was	less common in China.
The American diet		a healthy diet.
The Japanese diet		unhealthy.
		too much sugar.
		increasing in Japan.

Now take dictation. One of you will dictate 5 sentence from above while the other covers the boxes and writes below. Then change roles.

1. _____

2. _____

3. _____

4. _____

5. _____

READING 4

2–O   **Vocabulary review:** Organize these words into the two categories below. Then show a partner.

vegetables

sweets

cakes

pasta

meat

fish

fiber

eggs

rice

sugar

animal products

whole milk

ice cream

fruit

salt

grain

butter

cookies

cereal

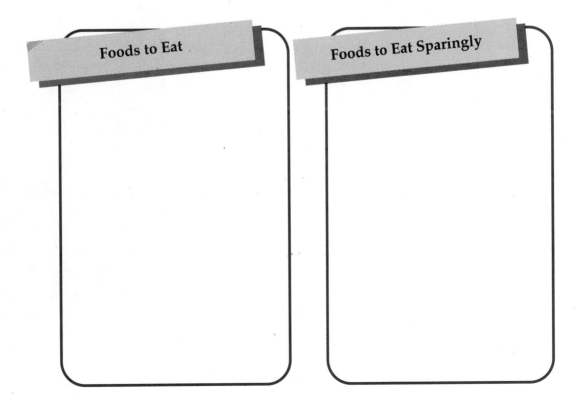

Foods to Eat

Foods to Eat Sparingly

READING 5: *Two For the Ages*

2–P   Long live Kin and Gin! Look at the picture, the title, and the subtitle of this article from *People* Magazine.

What do you know about these women?

Why are they stars in Japan? Read to find out.

TWO FOR THE AGES

Twin Centenarians Kin and Gin are Japan's Stars

1   Sometimes, fame and fortune like to wait. Kin Narita and Gin Kanie are twin sisters. They turned 100 in 1992. Their fame came recently when the
5   mayor of Nagoya honored them on Respect for the Aged Day. Then they began appearing in TV commercials. Now they are having the time of their lives selling everything from cosmetics to floor
10   mops. Reporters follow them everywhere, and a magazine pays them to give personal advice, including their thoughts on men. For the first time in their lives, they have enough money to file income tax
15   returns.

The sisters are proud of their big families: 10 children, 15 grandchildren, and 14 great-grandchildren. For entertainment, they watch TV. Gin likes politics while Kin
20   prefers wrestling. Although both can remember back to the 19th century, they do not romanticize the past. "Young people today are smarter," says Gin.

Gin (left) and Kin boast 10 children, 15 grandchildren and 14 great-grandchildren.

*From **People**, May 19, 1992 (adapted)*

This article doesn't tell why the twins have lived so long. With a group, write 5 possible reasons for their long life.

READING 6: *Why Women Live Longer than Men*

2-Q Look at the title of the article on the next page. With your class, try to predict some of the reasons why women live longer. Put your predictions on the board.

1

2

3

4

5

2-R Now read the article. Which of your predictions were confirmed? What new reasons did you learn? Write them here.

HOW YOU READ

Did predicting the article help your reading? Talk with the class about this.

READING 6

WHY WOMEN LIVE LONGER THAN MEN

1　Throughout the modern world, cultures are different, diets are different, and ways of life and causes of death are different. But one thing is the same—
5　women outlive men.

Some of the reasons are related to lifestyle. Men smoke more than women, and they drink more. They take more life-threatening chances. Men are mur-
10　dered more often than women (usually by other men). They commit suicide at a higher rate and have more **fatal** car accidents than women do. Men die more often in alcohol-related incidents.
15　Today, some scientists who study **longevity** believe that the data point to one conclusion: Mother Nature may **be partial to** women.

The reason may be **hormones.** Before
20　age 40, most women are still producing the female hormone estrogen. Heart disease kills only one woman in this age bracket for every three men in the U.S. After age 40, the **odds** in favor of women

25　drop. But they have an extra **decade** before their death rate from heart disease approaches that of men.

Not every difference between the sexes favors women. While women are
30　less vulnerable than men to life-threatening diseases, they are more **vulnerable** to everyday sicknesses and pain. Women take more medicine and spend more days in bed than men do. They suffer
35　from **arthritis, bladder** infections, **menstrual** pain, and migraine headaches.

In the meantime, men get heart attacks and **strokes.** Women are sick, but men are dead.
40　But behavior changes, so the health gap between men and women isn't a fixed feature of the landscape. Recently in the U.S., the gap has gotten smaller. Men are smoking less and eating better.
45　"The gap isn't shrinking because women are acting like men," says scientist Deborah Wingard. "It's shrinking because men are acting more like women."

From **Health,** *July/August, 1991 (adapted)*

---

fatal	resulting in death
longevity	long life
be partial to	like, favor
hormones	chemicals in the body
odds	advantages
decade	ten years
vulnerable	able to be injured or attacked
arthritis	inflammation of the joints
bladder	the bag in the body that holds urine
menstrual	having to do with the monthly discharge of the menses
strokes	sudden attacks of illness, usually with paralysis

READING 6

2–S Reread "Why Women Live Longer than Men." As you read, fill in the chart below.

> **READING STRATEGY**
> **After (or while) you read, you can try to make a chart to help you organize and remember information.**

Health Problems

WOMEN have more	MEN have more

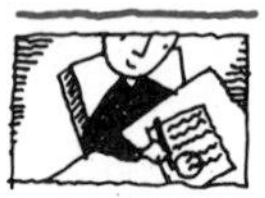

2–T **Independent Vocabulary Study:** Vocabulary Review and Word Forms. Turn to page 125 in the Vocabulary Appendix.

OPTIONAL READING 7: *Are You Cancer Prone?*

This quiz will help you evaluate your risk of developing cancer. Circle the points that apply to you. Write down your score for each section. Then add up your four scores and check the bottom of the page to see what your score means.

ARE YOU CANCER-PRONE?

1. Your Family History

+2 You have (had) one close relative with cancer.

+5 You have (had) more than one relative with cancer.

+10 You smoke and have one or more relatives with cancer.

+15 You smoke and have one or more close relatives with cancer and drink more than 3 ounces of alcohol a day.

+1 You drink more than 2 cups of coffee a day and have a close relative with pancreatic cancer.

SCORE #1 _____

2. Smoking and Environment

+1 You smoke, but less than 1 pack of cigarettes a day.

+5 You smoke 1 pack a day.

+10 You smoke 1 or more packs a day and drink more than 3 ounces of alcohol a day.

+2 You smoke cigars or a pipe.

+2 You live or work with smokers.

+3 You live and work with smokers.

+1 You live or work in an area with heavy air pollution.

+2 You live and work in an area with heavy air pollution.

SCORE #2 _____

3. Your Personal Habits

+3 You sunburn easily and have had a severe sunburn.

+2 You do not tan easily and are sometimes in strong sun.

+3 You are overweight by 20%.

+5 You are overweight by 25%.

+1 You have been overweight most of your life.

+2 You have been exposed to pesticides, toxic wastes, or asbestos.

+3 You have had many X-rays, especially when young.

+4 You drink more than 3 ounces of alcohol a day.

+2 You don't get regular, vigorous exercise.

+1 You often feel lonely.

+1 You have no close friends or relatives.

+1 You often feel depressed.

SCORE #3 _____

4. Your Diet

-5 You do not eat meat.

+1 You eat beef, pork or lamb 3 times a week.

+2 You eat beef, pork or lamb 5 times a week.

+3 You eat processed meats 3-5 times a week.

+4 You eat processed meats more than 5 times a week.

+2 You eat smoked or grilled foods more than once a week.

+1 You eat a lot of butter.

+1 You eat fried foods several times a week.

+2 You eat fried foods almost every day.

+1 You eat rich desserts or ice cream several times a week.

+2 You eat rich desserts or ice cream almost every day.

+1 You drink at least 2 glasses of whole milk every day.

+1 You eat cheese several times a week.

+2 You eat cheese almost every day.

+1 You eat sugary or processed foods several times a week.

+2 You eat sugary or processed foods almost every day.

+2 You eat less than 2 slices of whole-grain bread a day.

+3 You eat high-fiber cereal less than 3 times a week.

+3 You eat less than 3 servings of fruits or vegetables a day.

+3 You do not have orange juice or another citrus fruit every day.

+3 You eat broccoli, cabbage, cauliflower or Brussels sprouts less than 3 times a week.

SCORE #4 _____

TOTAL SCORE _____

From **Health Risks** *by Elliott J. Howard, M.D. and Susan A. Roth, 1987 (adapted).*

Your Cancer Risk-Factors Score

0 to 14	Low Risk
15 to 25	Moderate Risk
26 to 35	High Risk
36 +	Very High Risk

Of course, you can't alter your family history, but you can reduce your odds of developing cancer by improving your eating, drinking and life-style habits. Why not start to make positive health-enhancing changes today?

UNIT REVIEW: *Talk It Over*

We asked some international students *What do you do to stay healthy?* Here are their answers. Which student is most like you?

> I like swimming. Every week I swim 12 laps at the local pool. I try to eat good foods, but I don't always remember. To get away from the city and the bad air and stress, I often go horseback riding on weekends. On a horse, I become a different man.

Steve Gallegos is from Mexico.

> I have a healthy diet. I eat a lot of vegetables, fruit, and fish. I eat meat only twice a week. I sleep well, about 8 hours a night. I think it's also very important to laugh, and to take and give love.

Graciela Deoberti is from Argentina.

> To stay healthy, I try to avoid sugar as much as possible. So I always buy diet drinks and sugarless gum. And I make it a rule to drink two glass of orange juice every morning.
>
> Playing sports is an important thing for me. When I play, I enjoy myself. So I don't feel frustrated and uncomfortable. And I think that is the point of keeping healthy.

Michi Ishida is from Japan.

 Tell a partner which student is most like you. Explain why. Tell what you do to stay healthy.

 In your journal or elsewhere, write about what you do to stay healthy.

Fill in the chart below with names of classmates. Try to write a different name in each blank. To do this activity, you'll have to stand up and walk around the room. Ask questions such as

> *Do you like to walk?*

> *Do you eat meat?*

The first person to fill in all the blanks wins!

Find someone who . . .

likes to walk. _____

doesn't eat meat. _____

plays tennis. _____

drinks no alcohol. _____

doesn't smoke. _____

eats rice every day. _____

loves vegetables. _____

doesn't eat sugar. _____

exercises at least 3 times a week. _____

doesn't drink coffee. _____

rides a bike to school. _____

eats a good breakfast every morning. _____

UNIT REVIEW *Writing*

With a group or the class, write a letter and ask for up to 25 of any of these health brochures. Address the letter to *S. James, Consumer Information Center-Z, P.O. Box 100, Pueblo, CO 81002*

Include a check for $1.00 for each made out to *Superintendent of Documents.*

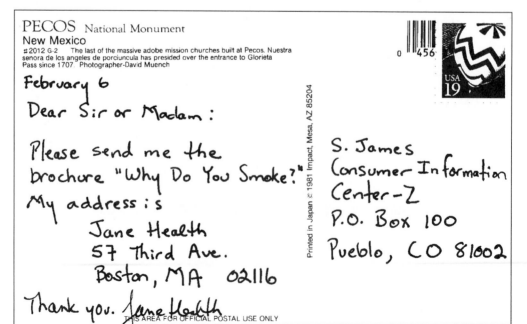

PECOS National Monument
New Mexico
#2012 G-2   The last of the massive adobe mission churches built at Pecos. Nuestra senora de los angeles de porciuncula has presided over the entrance to Glorieta Pass since 1707. Photographer-David Muench

Printed in Japan © 1981 Impact, Mesa, AZ 85204

February 6

Dear Sir or Madam:

Please send me the brochure "Why Do You Smoke?"
My address is
    Jane Health
    57 Third Ave.
    Boston, MA   02116
Thank you. *Jane Health*

S. James
Consumer Information
Center-Z
P.O. Box 100
Pueblo, CO 81002

THIS AREA FOR OFFICIAL POSTAL USE ONLY

UNIT REVIEW: *Information Tree*

Bring this tree to life! Add some leaves that tell what you remember from this unit.

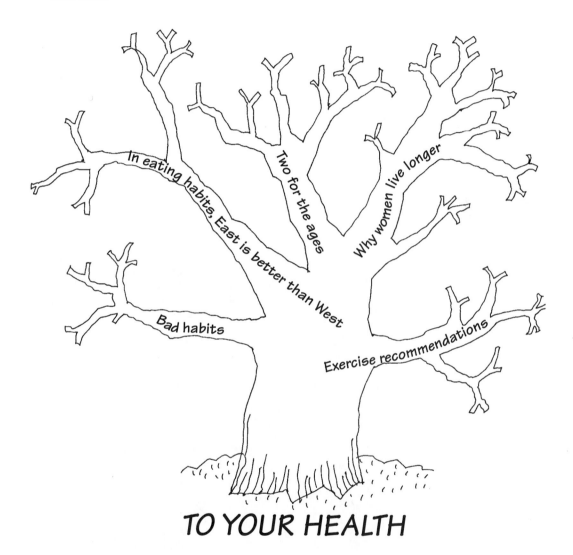

In eating habits, East is better than West

Two for the ages

Why women live longer

Bad habits

Exercise recommendations

TO YOUR HEALTH

Now compare your tree with a partner's.

UNIT REVIEW: *Word Power*

Fill in this crossword puzzle. All the words appeared in this unit.

Across

4. Kin and Gin's country
5. Kin and Gin are _____
9. Men do this more than women
10. Women have more of this than men
11. Biting your nails is a bad _____
12. A common food in China

Down

1. Someone who lives 100 years
2. The number of children Kin and Gin have
3. An exercise that requires no equipment and that anyone can do
6. The opposite of "poverty"
7. You should eat this sparingly
8. A country where people eat too much meat

Check your answers in the Answer Appendix on page 141.

3

Family Ties

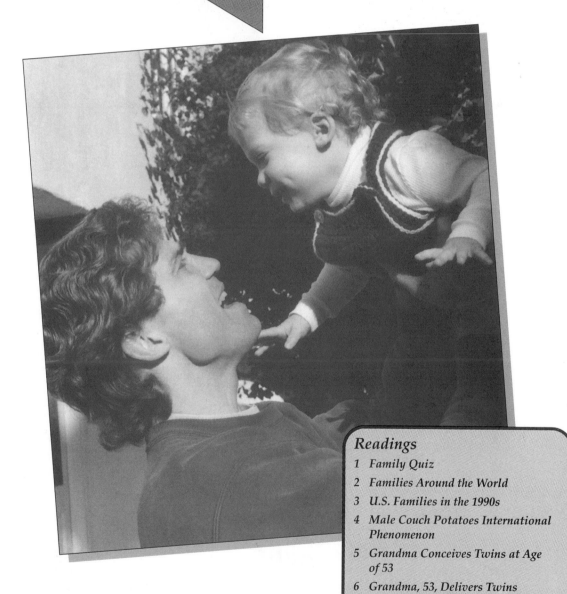

WARMING UP: *Talking about families*

3–A Work with a partner. Ask these questions:

Are families in your country similar to families in North America?

Are families or family roles changing in your country?

3–B Write down any words or phrases that you associate with the word "family." Share your ideas with the class.

_____

_____

_____

_____

_____

_____

3–C Which of these words do you associate with family? Circle them. Then tell why.

laugh quiet technology

food

changing trouble

money comfortable

work loud

responsibility

obey music

argue relax happy

READING 1: *Family Quiz*

 3–D How much do you know about families? With a partner, decide if these sentences are true or false.

Family Quiz

T F 1. In most families around the world, women work longer hours than men.

T F 2. The duties and expectations of parents and children within a family are similar around the world.

T F 3. Medical technology has now made it possible for women over 50 to have children.

T F 4. Over half of all marriages in the U.S. end in divorce.

T F 5. In Latin America, men work six hours less per week than women, on the average.

3–E Now look at the next page and check your answers.

How many did you get correct? _____

READING 1

Answers to family quiz

1. *True.* A recent study found that in most places around the world, women work more hours a week. To find out more about this study, see Reading 4.

2. *False.* To read about some differences between U.S. families and families in Asia, see Reading 2.

3. *True.* Women can now become pregnant after **menopause.** Read about one of the oldest women to become pregnant with the help of medical technology in Readings 5 and 6.

4. *True.* For more information and **statistics** about U.S. families in the 1990s, see Reading 3.

5. *True.* In Latin America, men work 54 hours, on the average, for every 60 hours that women work. You'll find more of these statistics in Reading 4.

✱
   menopause   the time of life when a woman's monthly period stops
     statistics   numbers that give information

READING 2: *Families Around the World*

3–F How are families the same or different in the U.S. (or Canada) and your country? Underline the choice that matches your opinion.

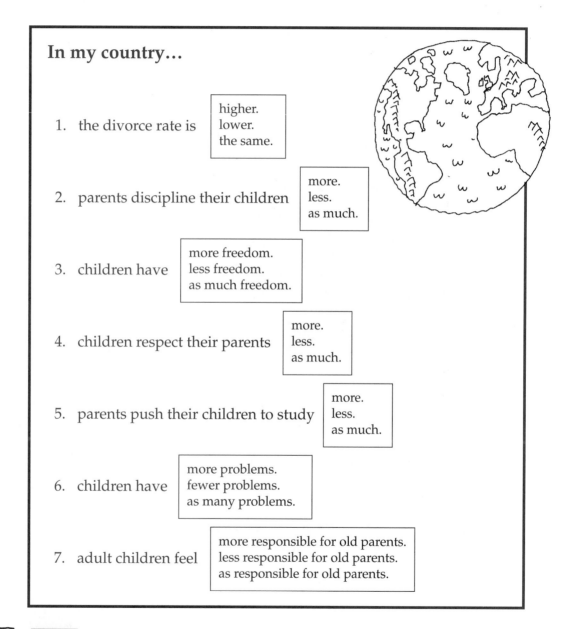

In my country...

1. the divorce rate is | higher. / lower. / the same.

2. parents discipline their children | more. / less. / as much.

3. children have | more freedom. / less freedom. / as much freedom.

4. children respect their parents | more. / less. / as much.

5. parents push their children to study | more. / less. / as much.

6. children have | more problems. / fewer problems. / as many problems.

7. adult children feel | more responsible for old parents. / less responsible for old parents. / as responsible for old parents.

3–G In a small group, discuss your opinions. Exchange information about families in your countries.

READING 2

3–H   We asked two international students to compare families in their countries with families in the U.S. Choose *one* text to read.

Do you agree with the writer's view of U.S. families?

This is Heasoon Noh, from Korea. She writes about parents and teens in the two countries.

In my country, parents sacrifice everything for their children, and they are very stern with them. Parents put a lot of pressure on their children to study hard. They think that studying will make the children successful. In fact, many teenagers study 13 or 14 hours a day. They are not allowed to date, and they have little time for activities like sports or music.

I've noticed that in the United States, parents think their own life is as important as their children's life. They have more freedom, and they give their children more freedom too. Parents let their children stay alone or relax after school, and they think it's natural for their teenagers to date.

Xen Pao Chen is from China. She writes about divorce rates and old people in the two countries.

In China, when two people get married and have children, they stay together. They never go away. It is their duty to teach and take care of their children. But in Europe and America, if parents don't get along, they don't think about their children and they separate. The divorce rate is much higher than in China.

Another difference between families in China and America is that Chinese children always take care of their old parents. If they don't take care of them, friends and colleagues will gossip about them. Chinese society condemns this kind of behavior, and sometimes newspapers even write about children who neglect their old parents. But in the United States, adult children often put their parents in a nursing home, and this is seen as a normal, customary thing to do.

3–1   Find one or two classmates who read the text that *you did not read*. Summarize for each other what you read and give your opinion about the text.

READING 3: *U.S. Families in the 1990s*

3–J   Look at the title of the text on the next page. What will the text be about? Make some predictions.

3–K   Now read the text as quickly as you can to get the main ideas; don't worry about the details.

Tell a partner what you understood.

> **READING STRATEGY**
>
> Good readers focus on major ideas the first time they read a difficult text.

3–L   Reread the text more carefully. As you read, fill out the chart.

U.S. Family Life in the 1950s and Early 1960s	U.S. Family Life Now
mothers often stayed home	*mothers often work*

> **READING STRATEGY**
>
> When a text compares two things, making a chart like this will help you read and remember.

READING 3

U.S. Families in the 1990s

1   American culture changed **radically** in the 1960s. The Sixties **glorified** personal freedom and attacked authority and convention, including traditional family life. The new search for individual happiness **set the stage** for sweeping changes in U.S. family life.

5   The typical nuclear family of the 1950s and early 1960s, with its working father and stay-at-home mother, is no longer typical at all.

In the 1990s, the typical mother is more likely to be out in the work force. She is working for personal satisfaction or economic reasons or, more probably, a combination of the two. With mother and father both

10   working, children of the Nineties spend more time alone and unsupervised. Many come home from school to an empty house. Child experts such as Dr. Benjamin Spock worry about the disappearance of **discipline** in families where working parents have limited time for their children. "Parents don't want to spend the little time they have with

15   children **reprimanding** them," says Spock.

Another change is that the number of single-parent families, especially those with women at the head, has increased dramatically. This is because about 60% of all marriages in the U.S. now end in divorce, and the majority of people who divorce have children under 18. Also, births

20   for unmarried—mainly teenage—mothers have risen sharply. While in 1950 only 4% of American children were born to unmarried women, in 1990 the figure was 27%. As a result, more and more American children are living in fatherless homes.

One positive change in the U.S. is in the new roles for men in the

25   family. Many fathers are present at the birth of their babies today. (Thirty years ago most were not.) And they are more willing to change **diapers** and cook dinner. It is no long seen as unmasculine to care for children and do household chores.

Who knows what further changes are in store for the U.S. family in

30   the next millennium?

---

*

radically	greatly
glorified	worshipped, honored
set the stage	prepared
discipline	a system of rules to keep order
reprimanding	verbally punishing
diapers	a baby's underwear

READING 3

3–M   **Independent Vocabulary Study:** Word Forms. See page 128 in the Vocabulary Appendix.

3–N   How is the family life in your country similar to or different from family life in the U.S.? Complete the chart, using information from Reading 3 or from your own personal experience.

	Similar to U.S.	Different from U.S.	How?
Divorce Statistics			
Single-Parent Families			
Raising Children			
Having Babies			
Women and Work			
Men and Housework			

Discuss your chart with a small group or the class.

3–O   In your journal or elsewhere, write about families in your country.

READING 4: *Male Couch Potatoes International Phenomenon*

3–P   In a small group, talk about your families and housework. In your homes, who does the following chores? Fill in the chart with your group. (For *cooking,* for example, if everyone in your group says "men," write "men." If some people say "men" and some people say "women," write "both," and so on.)

Household Chores	Men or Women or Both?
cooking	
shopping for groceries	
washing the car	
washing the dishes	
paying the bills	
making the beds	
washing the clothes	
caring for children	
taking out the garbage	
repairing broken things	
sweeping the floors	
cleaning the bathroom	
gardening	

What chores do women seem to do more often?

What chores do men seem to do more often?

READING 4

3–Q   Look at the headline on the opposite page. A *couch potato* is someone who spends a lot of time sitting on the couch and watching TV. What will the article probably tell you?

Read the large print under the headline. Does this information surprise you?

3–R   Does the article say anything about men and women in your country (or region of the world)? Scan it quickly, and underline the reference.

> **READING STRATEGY**
>
> Sometimes a reader wants to know if a text has a specific piece of information in it. The reader's eyes jump around the text to find it. This is *scanning*. What kinds of texts do you usually scan?

3–S   Now skim the article quickly for the main ideas. With your group, decide what the main ideas are.

> **READING STRATEGY**
>
> Sometimes a reader is interested in getting only the general ideas in a text. The reader reads the entire text rapidly. This is *skimming*.

*
phenomenon	a fact or circumstance
inequity	a lack of justice
hacienda	Spanish for "home"
domestic	related to the home
Nordic	Northern European
chore	a small job
butt	an object of ridicule or anger
gap	a space or distance
widening	getting larger
decade	a ten-year period

READING 4

Male Couch Potatoes International Phenomenon

THE ASSOCIATED PRESS

Nearly everywhere in the world, women work harder and earn less than men, and the gap in many countries is widening, the report says.

WASHINGTON—From Havana to Oslo to Warsaw to Tokyo to your hometown, the complaint is the same: Men aren't doing enough housework.

The problem of women having to dress the kids, wash the clothes, cook the meals, make the beds and take out the garbage—all before they go to work to earn less than men—is a worldwide **inequity,** according to an International Labor Organization report.

Even in Cuba, where a law requires men to help around the **hacienda,** 82 percent of all Havana women do all the **domestic** chores, says the report.

In **Nordic** countries, when men's working hours were reduced, they used the extra time for leisure activities rather than for housework or child care.

"In Poland, even the youngest of married men do not help with the housework, while Japanese men spent only 15 minutes a day on chores around the house," the report by the U.N. agency says.

"Couch potato" husbands, who sit like vegetables and watch television while wives do the **chores,** have been a longtime **butt** of jokes and feminine anger in the United States.

Nearly everywhere in the world, women work harder and earn less than men, and the **gap** in many countries is widening, the report says.

"Family responsibilities are at the heart of much discrimination against women," said Michel Hansenne, ILO director-general in Geneva, Switzerland. "Women are expected to stay at home to look after children and are then treated as second-class workers because of this."

The differences between pay for men and women is **widening** in both developing and industrialized countries, despite **decades** of efforts to push female equality on the job, the report says.

Women work more hours a week, including housework, than men in every part of the world except North America and Australia, the ILO report estimates.

They work the hardest in Africa. The report estimates that African women work 67 hours a week, compared to 53 for men. In Asia, women work 62 hours while men average 48 hours a week.

In North America and Australia, men work 49 hours a week, while women work 47.5, the report says. In Western Europe, women average 48 hours, men 43; Japan's women work 56 hours and men 54; in Latin America, women work 60 hours to 54 for men.

From **The New Mexican,** *September 7, 1992.*

READING 4

3–T   Do a more careful reading of the text. This time, look for specific information. Fill out the chart.

Hours of Work Per Week		
Place	Women	Men
Africa	*67*	*53*

> **READING STRATEGY**
>
> **Making a chart like this can sometimes help you organize, understand, and even remember a text.**

Write a short response to the information in the chart. Tell what you notice or think about the information. Share your response with a partner or the class.

READER RESPONSE

READING 4

3–U   We asked some international students: *Are men in your country couch potatoes?* This is what they wrote.

Which situation is closest to the situation in your country?

> In my country, the older generation helps out at home, but they won't admit it to their friends. It would ruin their "macho" image.
>
> Men of my generation, however, are not embarrassed about doing the housework. We sometimes even brag about being so helpful around the house.
>
> This differs, of course, from town to town and from family to family. One can feel the changes, though. Slowly but surely, the spirit of equality penetrates the minds of all men.

Lazar Dimitrijev is from the former Yugoslav Republic of Macedonia.

Rina Martemianova is from Russia.

> In Russia, wives and daughters usually do almost all domestic chores. Russian husbands and sons think that cooking is a female job. They come to the kitchen only to eat. Here in the U.S. I see many men who are able to cook.

> No! The average Romanian man doesn't have time to be a "couch potato." Because women are supposed to be equal to men, men have to help them with their work. And Romanian men really do it. Most help their wives with housecleaning, shopping, babysitting and even with washing and cooking! No, Romanian men don't have time to be "couch potatoes."

Nicolae Coman is from Romania.

In a small group, tell about men's and women's roles in your country. Compare your experiences with those of the students above.

READING 5: *Grandma Conceives Twins at Age of 53*

3–V Look at the headline, the photo, and the photo caption on the opposite page. What do you already know about the woman in the picture?

Her name is Mary Shearing.

What else do you want to know about this woman or this story? With the class, write questions.

<table>
<tr><td>

READING STRATEGY

Asking yourself questions before reading can help you concentrate and comprehend.

</td><td>

Question:

</td></tr>
</table>

Question:

Question:

Now read and underline any answers you find. Also, add more information about Mary Shearing in the box above.

READING 5

Grandma Conceives Twins at Age of 53

THE ASSOCIATED PRESS

1 ANAHEIM, Calif.—Mary Shearing is a 53-year-old grandmother and one of the oldest women to become pregnant with the help of medical technology. She says that nothing she
5 does surprises her family and friends anymore.

Seven years ago the athletic woman, who is an **avid** skier and former **amateur** body builder, married a man 21 years younger. And Monday she told reporters and television cameras that in
10 December she will give birth to twins.

Officials at Martin Luther Hospital here believe Shearing, who already has three grown children and two grandchildren by a previous marriage, is the oldest woman to achieve a dou-
15 ble pregnancy with a new technique that helps older women **conceive** even after **menopause.**

By this technique, eggs **donated** by a younger woman are **fertilized** with the sperm of the patient's mate. Then the eggs are implanted in
20 her **uterus.** An older woman's primary **obstacle** to getting pregnant, doctors say, is not the aging of her uterus but the aging of her eggs.

Dr. David G. Diaz, director of Martin Luther's reproductive medicine program, said
25 that four fertilized eggs were implanted in Shearing's uterus on May 15 and two have **survived.**

Most of the handful of older women who have become pregnant by this method have
30 chosen **anonymity.** But Shearing said that she wanted other middle-aged women who have struggled **in vain** to become pregnant to know they have an **option.**

She said that since she and her husband, Don
35 Shearing, were married, it has been their "dream" to have children.

Mary Shearing, 53, pregnant with test-tube twins, smiles during a press conference Monday in Anaheim, Ca.

From **The New Mexican,** *October 6, 1992 (adapted).*

avid	very eager; enthusiastic
amateur	nonprofessional
conceive	get pregnant
menopause	the female change of life
donated	given
fertilized	made fertile or productive
uterus	the place in a woman's body where a baby develops
obstacle	something that gets in the way
survived	continued to live
anonymity	the state of not revealing a name
in vain	with no result
option	choice

READING 5

3–W Write a short response to the article on the previous page. Tell what you notice or think about it. Share your response with a partner or the class.

3–X **Independent Word Study:** Word Forms. See page 131 in the Vocabulary Appendix.

READING 6: *Grandma, 53, Delivers Twins*

3–Y   The article on the next page appeared in the news five weeks after "Grandma Conceives Twins at Age of 53." Some of the original information is repeated, but much is new.

As you read, put a check (✓) next to information that is new. Then write down the most important new information here, in note form.

Share your notes with a partner or group.

3–Z   What new words do you want to remember from the text? Circle them and then write them in your Word Bank.

READING 6

Grandma, 53, Delivers Twins

Mary Shearing hopes to set an example for older women.

THE ASSOCIATED PRESS

1   ANAHEIM, Calif.—Twin test-tube girls born to a 53-year-old woman are "beautiful, absolutely fantastic" and should **inspire** oth-
5   ers who have difficulty having children, their father said Wednesday.

"I feel like a **proud** dad, very proud," Don Shearing, 32, said at a news conference at Martin Luther Hospital, where the girls were born prematurely Tuesday.

10   The girls' mother, Mary Shearing, was in good condition and good spirits, her husband said. Mrs. Shearing has three grown children by a previous marriage and two grandchildren. The twins are Don Shearing's first chil-
15   dren. About 12 weeks **premature,** they were in stable condition, said Dr. Leonard Fox, a neonatologist.

One child, 2-pound, 2-ounce Amy Leigh, was breathing with a ventilator. Her sister, 2-
20   pound, 12 1/2 ounce Kelly Ann, was breathing on her own, said Fox. "Everything looks great," said Fox. "The chance of survival now is excellent."

The twins were conceived using sperm
25   from her husband of seven years and eggs from an unidentified **donor** in her 20s who was paid $1,500, doctors said.

Shearing said the couple decided to undergo **in-vitro** fertilization in part to set an
30   example for other older women and couples with problems having children. "There is hope that they, too, can experience a family

inspire	influence in a positive way
proud	feeling pleased with oneself
premature	arriving too early
donor	someone who donates or gives something
in-vitro	in a test tube
post-natal	after birth

and children because it is a fantastic experience," said Don Shearing.

35   He rejected criticism that his wife was too old to have children and noted that many older men become fathers.

"It's a double standard," said Don Shearing.

40   A study published recently said women over age 40 are just as successful at bearing healthy babies with donated eggs as younger women, as long as the eggs come from a younger donor.

45   Diaz said Mrs. Shearing was a good candidate for the procedure because she was physically fit. She is a former amateur body builder.

Shearing said he was paying the med-
50   ical bills from his savings. Diaz said the in-vitro procedure costs about $9,000,
55   plus the $1,500 to the egg donor, in addition to the usual costs for births and **post-**
60   **natal** care.

George Shearing.

From **The New Mexican,** *November 12, 1992 (excerpted).*

OPTIONAL READING 7: *A Family Story*

A Family Story

The writer grew up in Laos. He now lives in Lowell, Massachusetts.

My parents had a lot of kids. They couldn't raise us all, so we had to separate and go to live with different relatives. That way we could have something to eat growing up, and we could go to school instead of work in the fields. I don't know exactly how many brothers and sisters I have. When I was seventeen I tried to track them down, and I found two or three of them. Then after sixteen years I met my real mother again. She cried and told me she felt very, very sorry, but that she did the best thing she could do.

When I came to the USA, my sister tried to help me out. She told me she wanted one of my twins for her own. I told her I wanted to raise all my kids. I don't want them to separate. I want every kid with me, no matter where I go.

UNIT REVIEW: *Talk It Over*

Take a survey of some classmates. Find out which readings they liked most. To do this activity, you'll need to stand up and walk around the room. Ask questions such as:

Which reading did you like the most? Why?

Which reading did you find the most interesting? Why?

Which was your favorite reading? Why?

Classmate's Name	Reading Liked Most	Reason

When time is up, report back on your findings.

UNIT REVIEW: *Writing*

Complete the following ideas. Then share your writing with a partner or group.

1. In my country, parents _____

   _____ but in North America,

   parents _____ .

2. In my country, children _____

   _____ but in North America,

   children _____ .

3. In my country, teenagers _____

   _____ but in North America,

   parents _____ .

4. In my country, women _____

   _____ but in North America,

   teenagers _____ .

5. In my country, men _____

   _____ but in North America,

   men _____ .

UNIT REVIEW: *Information Tree*

Bring this tree to life! Add some leaves that tell what you remember from this unit.

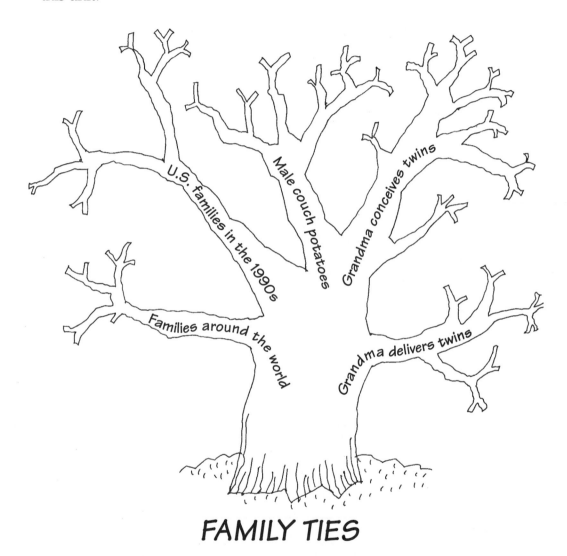

U.S. families in the 1990s

Male couch potatoes

Grandma conceives twins

Families around the world

Grandma delivers twins

FAMILY TIES

 Now compare your tree with a partner's.

UNIT REVIEW: *Word Power*

In each of the following groups, try to find one word that does not fit in with the others. Explain why.

Odd One Out	Reason
chore job housework (couch) clean make the bed	*All the other words are related to work.*
dad grandma husband twins test tube parent	
wife husband men male brother sons	
conceive birth baby deliver pregnant freedom	
babysit relax shop cook change diapers wash	
dating marriage kiss decade divorce separate	

4 ▶ Born to Shop

WARMING UP: *Talking about Shopping and Money*

4–A   Work with a partner. Ask these questions:

What do you like to spend money on?

What are your favorite stores? Why?

What material things can't you live without? (In other words, what things are necessary for your life?)

4–B   Write down any words or phrases that you associate with the idea of "money."

_____

_____

_____

_____

_____

_____

Share some with the class.

4–C   Which of these words do you associate with shopping? Circle them. Then tell why.

fun   headache   friends   clothes

CROWDS   MALL   happy

addiction

CREDIT-CARD   boredom   SPORTING GOODS

money

electronics   problems

READING 1: *Shopping Quiz*

4–D How much do you know about shopping? With a partner, decide if these sentences are true or false.

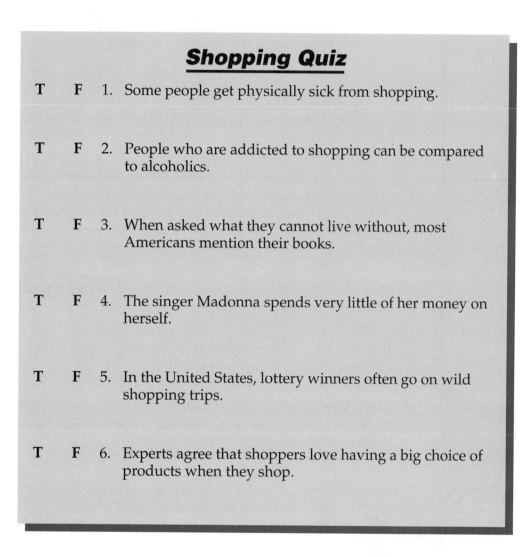

Shopping Quiz

T F 1. Some people get physically sick from shopping.

T F 2. People who are addicted to shopping can be compared to alcoholics.

T F 3. When asked what they cannot live without, most Americans mention their books.

T F 4. The singer Madonna spends very little of her money on herself.

T F 5. In the United States, lottery winners often go on wild shopping trips.

T F 6. Experts agree that shoppers love having a big choice of products when they shop.

4–E Now look at the next page and check your answers.
How many did you get correct? _____

READING 1

Answers to shopping quiz

1. *True.* Many people get headaches or become emotionally and physically exhausted from all the choices in the modern supermarket or shopping mall. See Reading 5 for further information.

2. *True.* Therapists at a New York psychiatric center treat compulsive shoppers as seriously as alcoholics or drug abusers. All have underlying problems. Reading 3 will tell you more about this addiction.

3. *False.* Many surveys over the years have asked Americans, "What can't you live without?" Books are not often mentioned, but videocassette recorders and Scotch tape are. Find out more about these surveys in Reading 2.

4. *False.* She spends an enormous amount of money on herself. Find out how much in Reading 4.

5. *True.* But some lottery winners give the money to others. Find out about lottery winners in Reading 6.

6. *False.* Many experts believe that the large amount of products in capitalist societies creates unnecessary stress for shoppers. For further information, see Reading 5.

READING 2: *Favorite Things, Timesavers All*

4–F   Think about the material things you own. Which things are essential for your life—so important that you cannot live without them? Make a list.

Things I Cannot Live Without

 Work with a group. Tell each other your lists. Below, write down all the things your group members mention. Which things were mentioned most often? Report back to the class.

READING 2: *Favorite Things, Timesavers All*

4–G　Preview the newspaper article on the next page. Look at the title, large type, and picture. Read the first paragraph. What will the article be about?

4–H　Skim the article quickly the first time for the general idea. Don't stop at new words; try to understand them from the context. Tell a partner what you understood.

Now read the text more carefully. This time, take notes on all the things North Americans can't live without.

Americans can't live without

Show your notes to a partner. Are the favorite things of Americans similar to your favorite things? Do you agree with the last paragraph?

4–I　**Independent Vocabulary Study:** Modifiers and nouns. Turn to page 133 in the Vocabulary Appendix.

READING 2:

Favorite Things, Timesavers All
By Alison Leigh Cowan

1 You would never find them in a survival kit, but they are the things Americans say they cannot live without: everything from microwave ovens 5 and videocassette recorders to Scotch tape and aluminum foil.

Until recently, experts say, the **fondness** that people expressed for certain items tended to correspond to how long 10 the items had been used in their homes.*

"It used to be, in order not to live without it, you had to live with it, for a while," said Dr. Steve Barnett, a cultural anthropologist at Holen North America, 15 a consumer research company in New York.

That has changed. The public's **appetite** for new products **emerges vividly** from consumer research done by 20 the Roper Organization, a public opinion research company in New York.

In a society full of households in which both partners work, anything that uses time more efficiently will **catch on** 25 rapidly.

That includes computers that allow executives to **squeeze in** a few hours of work before bedtime, videocassette recorders that let viewers skip commer-30 cials, and microwave ovens that can bake a potato in minutes.

"In the 1990s, time is the **scarce resource,** and the kinds of things people will not be able to live without will be 35 the kinds of things that free up time," Barnett said.

Libby Zurkow, 64, a real-estate broker in Wilmington, Delaware, is a case in point. The microwave oven she pur-40 chased seven years ago has meant she can prepare **drop-dead candlelight** dinners quickly.

"The greatest thing to have come along in modern times," she said of her 45 oven. "I just love great food, and I just don't have the time or interest to stay home all day."

Cars, followed by clothes washers, consistently lead Roper's must-have lists 50 for more than eight out of ten adults.

The bigger story, however, is how some new products are **capturing** consumers' **souls.**

Almost a quarter of the respondents 55 said they could not live without microwave ovens. It has taken other products many years to achieve such acceptance.

Sometimes it is the little things that 60 make life easier.

In the 1985 Roper survey, more people said they could not live without Scotch tape, no-iron cotton and aluminum foil than any of the other 20 65 items on the list.

This love affair with new products is not just an American phenomenon, experts say. Barnett said people in other cultures are just as dependent on new 70 products as Americans are.

* In other words, in the past, people said they liked their older possessions, not their new ones.

*From **The New York Times,***
May 10, 1989 (adapted)

---

*

fondness	love, affection	**scarce resource**	something valuable but limited
appetite	hunger	**drop-dead**	very elegant or special (slang)
emerges vividly	becomes very clear	**candlelight**	the light given by candles
efficiently	with very little effort or waste	**capturing**	taking by force or surprise
catch on	become popular	**soul**	the spiritual part of a person
squeeze in	fit (into a busy schedule)		

READING 3: *Compulsive Shopping Viewed as Addiction*

4–J   Have you ever bought something that you didn't need and didn't use? What was it? Why did you buy it? Tell classmates.

4–K   Look at the headline of this news article. What will it be about? Read the article and write a response to the story. (You can comment on the information in the text or tell what it makes you think of.)

READER RESPONSE

<table>
<tr><td>HOW YOU READ</td></tr>
<tr><td>Were you able to guess the meanings of any new words? Which ones?</td></tr>
</table>

Compulsive Shopping Viewed As Addiction

1   NEW YORK—A woman has 187 belts in her closets and drawers, most of them never worn or even looked at.

A man thinks only the most expen-
5   sive exercise bicycle will help enhance his physique, even though he already owns a lot of body-building equipment that he doesn't use.

Such people are compulsive spend-
10   ing addicts. Therapists at a New York psychiatric treatment center take the affliction as seriously as the problems of alcoholics and drug abusers.

"They think that owning things
15   makes them feel better," says Dr. Francesca Kress, director of psychological assessment at the Hapworth Centers in New York City.

"As their lives become more and
20   more of a disaster, they will treat themselves to something they can't afford," Kress says.

"When material objects are used as

Discuss your response with a small group. Then talk about anything you didn't understand in the article.

35   a way to make yourself feel better, there's a problem," according to Kress, who treats addicts at Hapworth's compulsive spending addiction program.

    "Rather than deal with the problem, they
40   think that they can go out and buy something to make themselves feel better," Kress says.

    "In our societies we're terribly materialistic—especially in North America," Kress points out. "We believe there's a God-given
45   right to acquire things, to be capitalistic. It's almost a holy thing."

    Hapworth's compulsive spending treatment program is one of several that the medical facility provides. It also runs programs for people
50   addicted to alcohol, drugs, and tobacco or people with eating disorders.

    A 90-minute behavior evaluation costs $150 and Hapworth charges $90 for a private behavior therapy session and $50 for group therapy.
55   The center says most insurance companies cover these costs.

    Besides helping patients stick to a budget and break their spending habits, Hapworth tries to get to the root of their problem.

From **St. Louis Post-Dispatch,** *October 1, 1989 (adapted).*

4–L   Look again at this article. Which new words would you like to learn and remember? Enter them into your Word Bank.

READING 4: *Madonna and Money*

4-M   What kind of spending habits do you have? Estimate how much money you spend on yourself each year in these categories.

Shoes   _____

Clothes   _____

Hair   _____

Jewelry, belts, and accessories   _____

4-N   Look at the text on the next page. Madonna spends a lot of money on herself. Appropriately, she is often called the "Material Girl" after her hit song by the same name.

Compare what you spend in each category with what Madonna spends. Write your opinion about her spending habits.

READER RESPONSE

READING STRATEGY

In North American schools, students are expected to give personal opinions about what they read. Is this true in your country?

4-O   Share your opinions with a group. Then discuss this question?

What annual salary do you need to be happy (in the U.S./in your country)?

READING 4: *Madonna and Money*

If you want to look like the Material Girl, you need lots of material things that cost plenty of money. How much? Below are some estimates of what Madonna spends on herself each year.

Clothes: $170,000
This would pay for
- 15 dressy outfits ($5,000 each)
- 25 day outfits ($3,500 each)
- $7,500 for basic clothes like jeans, T-shirts and sweatsuits

Hair: $4,500
This would pay for a $150 haircut every four weeks at a top beauty salon, and a hair color treatment ($150) every three weeks.

Jewelry: $20,000
This would pay for a supply of large bracelets, necklaces, cross pendants, sterling silver earrings, rings and belts such as Madonna wears.

Personal Training: $35,000
One expert suggests that to look like Madonna, you would need a personal trainer for two hours a day for three months to get into good shape. This would be followed by four hour-long sessions per week to maintain fitness.

Nails: $5,200
Weekly manicures and pedicures ($100 for both) are essential when you're a star.

Shoes: $20,000
You'll need at least forty pairs of boots, flats and heels (at an average of $500 a pair) to look like Madonna. You'll need 20 pairs for the East Coast and 20 pairs for the West Coast, so that you'll never have to pack shoes when you travel.

READING 5: *Overchoice*

4–P With a group, discuss these questions:

> *How is shopping in North America different from shopping in your country?*
>
> *What do you like or dislike about supermarkets and department stores here?*

4–Q Preview the following article. Look at the headlines, the photo, and the caption (the words under the photo). Write a general question you have about the topic.

Question:

> **READING STRATEGY**
>
> Asking yourself questions before reading can help you concentrate and comprehend.

Read the article quickly the first time to look for an answer to your question.

4–R Read a second time to find the opinions of all the people who are mentioned in the article. Categorize them below.

These People Dislike a Lot of Choice	These People Like a Lot of Choice

Which category does the writer belong in? Which category do you belong in? Discuss these questions with the class.

Overchoice

Some experts are beginning to wonder if 57 varieties of one item may be too much of a good thing.

"You can go into a major shopping mall and become emotionally exhausted in one hour."—JEREMY RIFKIN

By Beth Ann Krier

Rows upon rows of products make decision-making difficult for some shoppers.

1 Have you visited your local Cereal Aisle from Hell lately? Did trying to find the right **cereal** leave you confused?

Some supermarkets have more than 40 vari-
5 eties of cereal, and more are on the way.

You say you're getting a headache from just thinking about cereal choices? Trying to find a pain reliever could make your headache even worse. First, you have to know the difference
10 between aspirin, acetaminophen and ibuprofen. Then you have to decide if you want regular or extra-strength formula. Finally, you have to choose capsules, tablets, or caplets.

"There's just too many products for stores to
15 absorb. Companies have to cut back," explained Product Alert executive editor Tom Vierhile. "There's about a million cereals now. It's pretty amazing."

According to Rex Beaber, a Los Angeles clin-
20 ical psychologist, people can spend a large part of their lives making decisions about what to buy. Most of us already have busy lives, he points out, and it is stressful to spend extra time shopping.

25 Some shoppers, of course, don't mind this at all. Russian immigrant Anatoly Rosinsky, a musician in Los Angeles, recalls, "In Russia, you stand in line for half an hour to buy beer. Then you have one choice if they have beer
30 that day. Here, you spend 30 minutes deciding which beer to buy. In the end, you lose about the same amount of time. But this way it's much more pleasant."

But some people think there is a bigger prob-
35 lem than lost time: stress.

"You can go into a major shopping mall and become totally, emotionally **exhausted** in one hour. The reason is that there are too many items to pick from," says Jeremy Rifkin, president of
40 Foundation on Economic Trends.

Rifkin adds that **consumers** nowadays feel they have to consider environmental questions (such as whether the product is harmful to the environment). They also have to consider health
45 questions (such as whether the product contains harmful additives.)

"It's a tremendous emotional **burden**," he says, "well beyond the level of stress that our parents knew 20 years ago."

From **The Los Angeles Times,** *February 12, 1989 (adapted)*

---

*		
cereal	a popular breakfast food in the U.S. made from oats, corn, wheat, etc.
exhausted	very tired
consumers	people who buy goods and services
burden	a heavy load

READING 5

4–S   In a group, discuss the meaning of the following words and phrases. Don't use a dictionary. Try to write a word or phrase with a similar meaning.

If you didn't know these words and phrases before, what helped you understand them?

1. *cut back* (line 15)

2. *recalls* (line 27)

3. *pick from* (line 39)

4. *harmful additives* (line 46)

4–T   **Independent Vocabulary Study:** Word forms and prefixes. Turn to page 135 in the Vocabulary Appendix.

READING 5

4–U   Think about the choices in your life now. Are there too many? Too few? Just enough? Put a check (✓) next to your ideas. Then discuss the questionnaire with a partner.

Choices in My Life			
Choices	**Too Many**	**Too Few**	**Just Enough**
things to do on the weekend			
good TV programs to watch			
good movies to see			
restaurants in my town			
friends to call			
kinds of ice cream in the supermarket			
(other)			
(other)			

READING 6: *Winning the Lottery*

4–V If you won the lottery, how would you spend your money? What would you buy?

Preview the two articles and then choose *one* to read. How did the winner spend the money?

A Change of Heart

By Ron Arias

After winning the Lotto in Erie, PA, a new millionaire spends some of his money on the once hated Russians

O n a gray winter afternoon in Moscow, Ken Wayne of Erie, PA, sits with a glass of vodka and the Chekmariov family. "To the future of the new Russia—cheers!" says Wayne."

Two years ago, Wayne, 44, won $9.6 million in the Pennsylvania Lotto. "I was just another guy with
10 an impossible dream," he says.

Wayne rests on Moscow-bound supplies being loaded in Hartford, Conn.

"But it came true. Now I'm in Moscow with another dream." Wayne's dream? To help save Russia and its sister republics.

Wayne wasn't always so **ambitious.** Before winning the lottery, he lived in a small apartment and drove a rented van. Then,
15 on Feb. 6, 1990, he **hit the jackpot.** He stopped working almost at once. He bought two big homes and two fancy cars. He took a Caribbean cruise and got married.

But in 1992, Wayne's **carefree** lifestyle changed. Even though he had grown up hating the Soviet Union (his Polish grandpar-
20 ents detested the Communist regime in their native land), he was struck by something he saw on TV about the crisis in Russia. "There was an old man standing in a line. He was fighting for a little bag of butter," he recalls. "It was like he was grabbing for his life." **Haunted by** this image, Wayne decided to use some of
25 his lottery money to help the situation. He recently gave $100,000 to send two airplanes of food and medicine to Moscow. He has appeared on TV, asking other Americans to give money too. "It's time to turn old enemies into friends," he says. "I'm just glad I found a cause. I never thought I'd say it, but helping the Russians
30 gives me a **real high.**"

From **People,** *Feb. 3, 1992 (adapted)*

---

*

ambitious
  full of a desire to succeed

hit the jackpot
  won everything in the "pot"

carefree
  with no cares or worries

haunted by
  obsessed with; when you're haunted by something, you can't forget it

a real high
  (*slang*) a lot of happiness

4–W   Find one or two classmates who read the text that *you did not read*. Summarize for each other what you read. Then discuss this question: *Are the two lottery winners alike in any way?*

Helping Others

1   Curtis "Mack" Sharp of West Orange, N.J., a porter at AT&T Bell Laboratories near Short Hills, won $5.6 million in the New York lottery in 1982. He showed up at lottery headquarters to claim his prize with his **estranged** wife on one arm and his girl-
5   friend on the other, promising to share the **bonanza** with both. He provided his ex-wife with a trust fund that will make her a millionaire too. He presented his girlfriend with a $10,000 engagement ring and a $13,000 wedding dress, and married her in a $100,000 ceremony. He bought a $26,000 bronze Cadillac
10   with a $5,000 telephone and moved into a 14-room, $200,000 house with a cedar-lined closet for the new Mrs. Sharp's **furs.** Not surprisingly, Sharp's first check was quickly **gobbled up.**

Now that a bank manages his investments, Sharp is more **cautious**—and is helping others. He gave $15,000 to send sup-
15   plies to Ethiopia and is a fund raiser for other African relief groups. And through his church, he and his wife helped establish the largest shelter for homeless people in New Jersey.

20   Sharp is still working at Bell Labs so he can collect pension benefits when he retires. "This lottery thing was a
25   dream," he explains. "But the job is real."

From **Reader's Digest,** *August, 1986 (excerpted)*

Jackpot winner Curtis Sharp.

4–X   Look again at the text you read. Which new words would you like to learn and remember? Enter them into your Word Bank.

*
estranged
 separated
bonanza
 source of wealth
furs
 coats made from
 animal hair
gobbled up
 eaten up
cautious
 careful

OPTIONAL READING 7: *Material Things*

Material Things

Dominika Szmerdt is from Poland.

I have never been considered a materialistic person. As a child I didn't need expensive clothes and toys to have a good time with my friends. We used to play for hours using mostly our imagination and initiative. The "world of things" was simply not able to influence our world, full of fantastic creatures and events.

As I grew older, my attitude towards material things, and money in particular, remained similar. I could live without them easily, with maybe one exception— books. They were my only addiction, and I spent most of my pocket money on them.

As a young girl, I valued boys with a sense of humor and sensitivity more than those who could take me to an expensive restaurant in their car.

That's how it used to be. And now? As an adult I'm so preoccupied with saving money for my own apartment. There are so many things I just cannot do without—books, clothes, food, and travel. Of course supporting oneself is part of being an adult, but I have a feeling that my idealistic, "pure" world has been lost somewhere on the way to my adulthood.

I still believe that all the best things in life are free, but knowing that, I often repeat to myself, "Money cannot exactly buy you happiness, but at least it helps you suffer in comfort."

UNIT REVIEW: *Talk it Over*

Fill in the chart below with names of classmates. Try to write a different name in each blank. Stand up and walk around the room. Ask questions such as

Are you a compulsive shopper?

Do you find it stressful and exhausting to shop?

Find someone who...

is a compulsive shopper. _____

finds it stressful and exhausting to shop. _____

loves the choices in the supermarket. _____

spends more than $500 a year on clothes. _____

can't live without a VCR. _____

thinks Madonna's spending habits are wrong. _____

likes old things better than new. _____

hates to spend money. _____

thinks about environmental issues when shopping. _____

can't live without a computer. _____

wants to become less materialistic. _____

UNIT REVIEW: *Writing*

We asked some international students: *Are material things important to you?* Here are their answers. Which student is most like you?

> I want to get a car. And I want to help my family get a bigger house. I have five brothers, one sister, and my mom and dad. I want to make things good for them. That's why money is important to me.

Nancy Rascon is from Mexico.

Qatip Arifi is from Albania.

> For me personally, material things are very important. I work hard for them. But health and happiness are important too. My family is the most important of all. There is nothing in the world that I would compare with the smile of my children.

> Material things like fancy clothes and fast cars are of no importance to me. I don't evaluate people by their appearance or possessions. For example, I can talk to a person for hours without even noticing what this person is wearing. I only notice his character.

Biljana Shopova is from the former Yugoslav Republic of Macedonia.

Write your own answer to the question in your journal or elsewhere. Share your writing with classmates, if you wish.

UNIT REVIEW: *Information Tree*

Bring this tree to life! Add some leaves that tell what you remember from this unit.

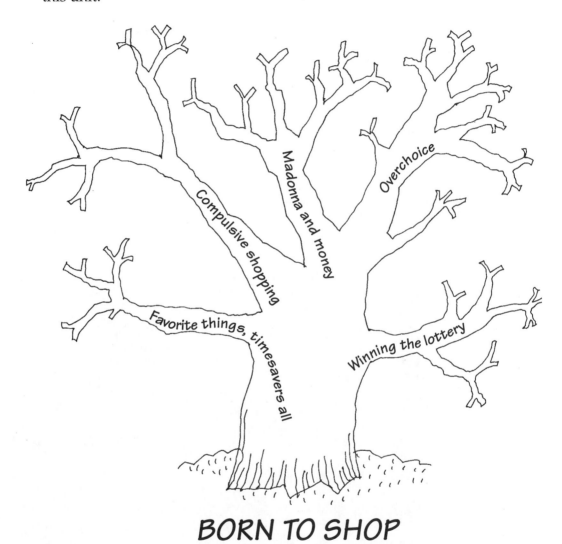

Madonna and money

Overchoice

Compulsive shopping

Favorite things, timesavers all

Winning the lottery

BORN TO SHOP

 Now compare your tree with a partner's

UNIT REVIEW: *Word Power*

Fill in the crossword puzzle. The words all appeared in this unit.

Across

1. The "Material Girl"
4. Many people feel there is too much of this in North American stores
6. Madonna's shoes _____ more than $20,000 a year
8. Busy people want to buy products that save _____
9. A person addicted to alcohol
10. Many people feel this when they shop

Down

2. Compulsive spenders are _____ to shopping
3. Things people cannot live without
5. Supermarkets have more than 40 varieties of this
6. Madonna spends about $170,000 a year on these
7. A person who shops

Check your answers in the Answer Appendix on page 142.

5

Going Places

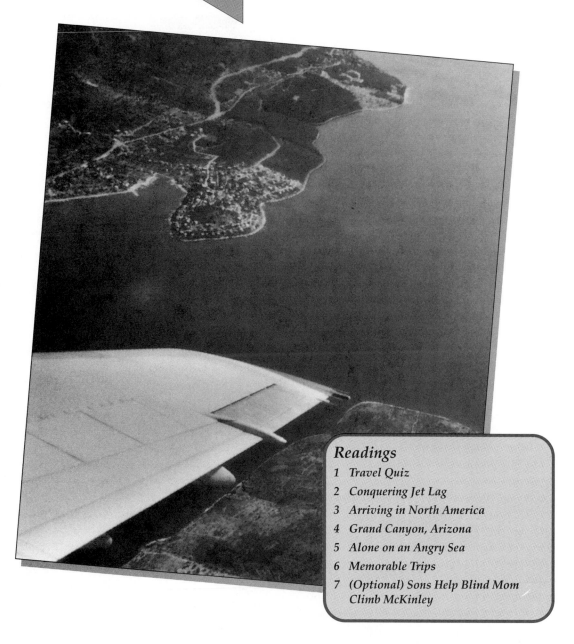

WARMING UP: *Going Places*

5–A   Work with a partner. Ask these questions:

> *Do you like to travel?*
>
> *What is the best trip you ever took? The worst?*

5–B   Write down any words or phrases that you associate with the words "travel" or "trip."

_____

_____

_____

_____

_____

_____

Share some of your words with the class.

5–C   Which of these words do you associate with your experience of travel? Circle them. Then tell why.

sad   nature   **happy**   boring

fear   **bike**

lost   **trouble**   jetlag

beach   money

mule   *difficult*   museums   **exciting**

READING 1: *Travel Quiz*

 5–D How much do you know about travel? With a partner, decide if these sentences are true or false.

Travel Quiz

T   F   1. When you fly long distances, it's a good idea to eat and drink frequently.

T   F   2. Traveling to a new country can be an exciting and wonderful adventure.

T   F   3. It is possible to cross the Pacific Ocean in a rowboat.

T   F   4. Tourists at the Grand Canyon can enjoy wonderful views only from the top of the canyon.

T   F   5. Traveling east by plane is more difficult than traveling west.

5–E Now look at the next page and check your answers.

How many did you get correct? _____

READING 1

Answers to travel quiz

1. *False.* Although it is a good idea to drink frequently, you'll feel better if you eat lightly and infrequently. It's hard to digest food when you're sitting still for a long time. For more advice on flying, see Reading 2.

2. *True.* Going to a new country can be a happy experience, but it can also be a time of confusion, surprise, or pain. See Reading 3 for two personal stories of arriving in North America.

3. *True.* Gerard d'Aboville rowed across the Pacific from Japan to the U.S. in 1991. He was lucky to survive. Read about his trip in Reading 5.

4. *False.* Tourists can travel to the bottom of the canyon on foot, on a **mule,** or by riverraft. The view from the bottom *is* wonderful. See Reading 4 for more information about trips to the bottom of the Grand Canyon.

5. *True.* Because of the body's internal clock, going east is harder than going west. See Reading 2 for more information on "jet lag."

*

| mule   the offspring of a horse and a donkey |

READING 2: *Conquering Jet Lag*

5–F   Answer these questions about travel.

What is your favorite way to travel?

_____ by bus

_____ by boat

_____ by car

_____ by plane

_____ by train

_____ (other) _____

How do you feel about flying?

_____ I've never flown.

_____ I like it.

_____ I'm afraid of it.

_____ I get air sick.

_____ It's a bother.

_____ I feel bad afterwards.

_____ (other) _____

Take a survey of the class.

How many people have flown? _____

How many people have felt jet lag? _____

Who has taken the longest trip by air? _____

How did this person feel afterwards? _____

5–G   With a group or partner, preview "Conquering Jet Lag" on the next page. Talk about the organization of the text. How many major parts are there? What are they?

READING STRATEGY

Many texts have organizational signals (for example, bold print) that can help you read. Look for them before you read.

READING 2

5–H Read the text below to find information that you didn't know before. Put a check (✓) next to new information.

CONQUERING JET LAG

1 Have you ever taken a long plane trip? How did you feel afterward? If you are like most people, you suffered from jet lag for a few days after the flight. Jet lag is the feel-
5 ing of fatigue and imbalance that is caused by traveling through several time zones so quickly. The body's internal, biological clock cannot adjust. Jet lag usually affects travelers going east more than those going
10 west.

There are some simple strategies to help fight jet lag. Experts offer the following advice:

Before You Go
15 ● *Get plenty of sleep before the trip.*
● *Dress comfortably.* Don't wear high heels, tight clothes, or neckties. A running suit is a good travel outfit.

In the Air
20 ● *Get comfortable.* Take your shoes off and put on a pair of slippers or heavy socks. Ear plugs and an eye mask can help you sleep.

Traveling Through Time

WEST←   → EAST

● *Drink plenty of liquids.* The dry, pres-
25 surized air in planes can cause dehydra-tion. Try to drink a glass of water every hour. Don't drink alcohol or coffee, since these liquids accelerate dehydration.
● *Don't overeat.* It's hard for the body
30 to digest food while sitting still. Vegetarian foods will be easier for you to digest than meats.
● *Move about the plane.* This will increase your circulation and help prevent
35 swelling in your ankles and feet. Try to do simple stretching exercises in your seat.
● *Sleep as much as possible.* Especially if you're flying east, go to sleep as early as possible. Don't stay up for the movie, and
40 try not to stay up for dinner.

After You Arrive
● *Spend time outside.* Studies show that exposure to strong light can help workers adjust to new work schedules. Experts
45 think that strong light can help jet lag suf-ferers too.
● *Reset your watch on the plane.* Get on the schedule of the local people as quickly as possible.

Tell a partner what new information you learned.

HOW YOU READ

Is it helpful to talk with other readers about a text?

READING 2

5–I   Work with a partner. Practice making true sentences using the words and phrases in the boxes. Can you each make 3 sentences? Note that this is a *speaking* activity.

Conquering Jet Lag

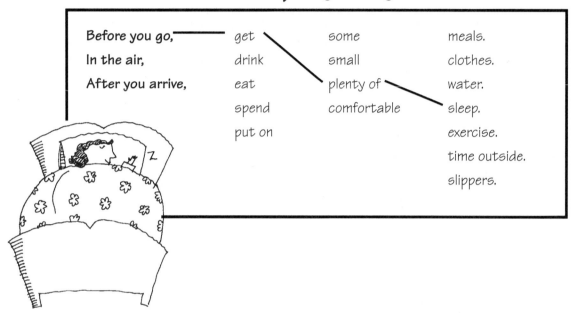

Before you go,	get	some	meals.
In the air,	drink	small	clothes.
After you arrive,	eat	plenty of	water.
	spend	comfortable	sleep.
	put on		exercise.
			time outside.
			slippers.

Now take dictation. One of you will dictate 4 sentences from above while the other covers the boxes and writes below. Then change roles.

1. _____

2. _____

3. _____

4. _____

5–J   **Independent Vocabulary Study:** Verbs indicating change; Vocabulary review. Turn to page 137 in the Vocabulary Appendix.

READING 3: *Arriving in North America*

5–K   Do you remember your first days in North America (or in another new country or city)? What happened? How did you feel? Tell a partner.

5–L   Here, Maniya Barredo, a ballerina from the Philippines, tells about her first days in New York. In the text on the next page, Liu Zongren, a journalist from China, describes his first days in Washington, D.C. Choose one text to read. Did you experience any of the same things as the writer?

> **READING STRATEGY**
>
> Good readers link what they read with their own experience.

Maniya Barredo. Born in Manila, Philippines, Ballerina.

I arrived in New York from Manila, alone but **exhilarated.** I was eighteen on my first big trip away from home. My uncle was to meet me at the airport, but I couldn't find him in the crowd.

I saw some people getting into a long black limousine, so I went up to the driver with a slip of paper that my parents had given me. I said, "I want to go to this address." I had no idea where it was. My parents told me that my uncle lived somewhere in Queens, not more than twenty minutes from the airport.

The driver dropped people off at different locations. After a long ride, I was the last person in the back seat of the car. All of a sudden, the driver parked in a dark, secluded place. I didn't have much life experience, but I had enough sense to know that I was in trouble.

I started crying uncontrollably. I said, "I just arrived in this country. Please, don't hurt me." It was horrible. Thank God, the man had some **compassion.** I was able to reason with him, and he took me to my uncle's home. That was my first day in America.

The next day, I was supposed to **audition** at the American Ballet Center, on 8th Street and Avenue of the Americas in Manhattan. Well, my uncle put me on a subway in Queens and said to get off at West 4th Street. I had never ridden on public transportation in the Philippines. I always traveled by car. I didn't even know what riding in a bus was like. But there I was on the **frantic** New York subway. I was **petrified.** And I was too shy to ask anyone for directions. I missed my exit and went all the way to God knows where.

At the end of the line, I was the only person left on the train. I pulled my rosary out of my purse and began praying. Finally the train started back toward Manhattan. Eventually I found West 4th Street.

From **New Americans: An Oral History** *(excerpted)*

---

*

exhilarated	very happy and lively
compassion	sympathy, pity
audition	take a test of one's dancing or acting ability
frantic	excited, wild
petrified	very afraid; frozen with fear

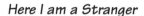

Liu Zongren. Born in Beijing, China, Journalist.

Here I am a Stranger

After a flight of twenty-two hours, we crossed over the coast of the United States and prepared for our landing at Dulles International Airport in Virginia, twenty miles west of Washington, D.C. We were all exhausted as we climbed aboard the bus. We were met by representatives of the Chinese Embassy, who drove us to the embassy where we were to stay for ten days.

While the other members of our group stayed busy, taking tours and exploring the beautiful capital of the richest country in the world, I stayed alone, feeling sad. I was suffering from jet lag and nostalgia, missing my family. It was during these days that I wrote my wife Fengyun my first letter from America:

The temperature is much the same here as in Beijing. The difference is that everywhere there is green grass. There are no crowds of people on the street. The stores are quiet and empty most of the time. I don't know how they make a living selling so little.

Our son would like this place; there are squirrels everywhere! You don't feel squeezed in as we do on Beijing streets. There is so much space. In the windows of stores, TVs are on all day and night. Nobody bothers to turn off the lights even during the day.

Cars and more cars—as many cars as we have bicycles. Very few people walk. There are also very few public buses. Most people drive cars, even old women drive.

At the embassy kitchen we have chicken every meal. We could have a whole chicken if we could eat it. We have apples, oranges and bananas at every meal, plenty of them. Plenty of milk. They say Americans drink milk like we drink water. But I have little appetite. This may be caused by jet lag, but I think the real reason is that I don't feel comfortable here.

From **Two Years in the Melting Pot** (excerpted)

---

exhausted	very tired
nostalgia	homesickness
squirrels	small animals with bushy tails

5–M Find one or two classmates who read the text that *you did not read.* Summarize for each other what you read. Then discuss this question: *Are Maniya's and Liu's experiences similar in any way?*

5–N Look again at the text you read. Which new words would you like to learn and remember? Enter them into your Word Bank.

READING 3

5–O Walk around the room and ask the following question of five classmates. Take notes on their answers.

What surprised or confused you when you first arrived in North America?

Classmates' Names	Thing(s) That Surprised or Confused

Tell a partner what you learned, and then report back to the class.

5–P In your journal or elsewhere, write about your first days in North America (or in another new country or city).

READING 4: *Grand Canyon, Arizona*

5–Q   What is the most interesting place you've seen in North America (or in the world)? What was special about it? Tell your classmates. Below, write the names and locations of the places that your classmates mention.

5–R   The Grand Canyon is one of the most popular tourist destinations in North America. What do you know about it? Brainstorm with a group. Write the information below.

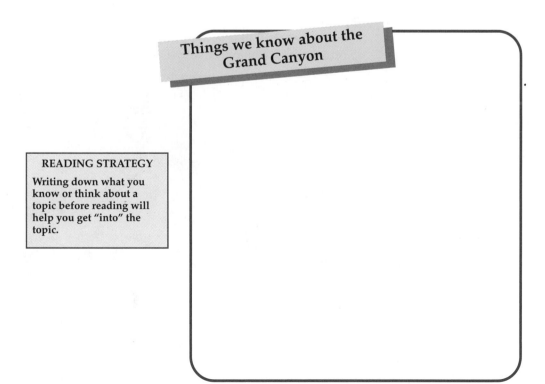

Things we know about the
Grand Canyon

READING STRATEGY

Writing down what you know or think about a topic before reading will help you get "into" the topic.

READING 4

5–S Preview this travel article. Look at the pictures, title, subheadings, and first paragraph. What will it be about?

Now read the article to see which trip you would prefer to take.

Tell a partner which trip you prefer. Why?

Grand Canyon, Arizona

1 Most visitors to the two-billion-year-old Grand Canyon see it from the rim. It's a breathtaking sight, with its unbelievable size, spectacular colors, and the Colorado River snaking below. But if you want a truly memorable adventure, you should take
5 one of two special trips that let you "live" the Grand Canyon experience from the bottom.

By Riverraft

If you are especially adventurous, a three-day rafting trip down the mighty Colorado River will delight you. You'll feel
10 the power of the river that carved out the canyon. The **swift currents** punctuated by thunderous **rapids** will give you the ride of your life. When your heart is not in your throat and your mind not on survival, your eyes will take in the grandeur of the walls rising up around you. At night, you will camp on
15 the banks of the river, cook over an open fire, and rediscover the stars.

By Mule

If you prefer to stay on dry ground, you can take an overnight mule trip to the bottom of the canyon. As you

The Colorado River offers plenty of excitement.

5–T   Work with a group to discuss the meaning of the following words. Use the context to help you.

carved out (line 10)   *thunderous* (line 11)   *descend* (line 20)

graze (line 21)   *clutch* (line 23)   *race* (line 25)

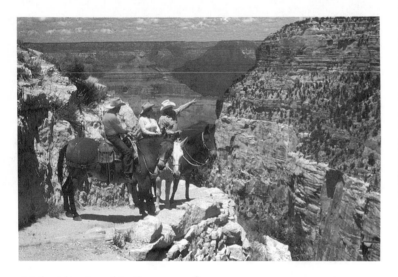

Mule riders travel to the canyon floor.

5–U   If you wish, write a letter or make a toll-free call to get more information about these trips.

20 descend, the magical colors of the canyon walls surround you. **Bighorn sheep** graze on ledges. Pine trees, **cacti,** and wildflowers decorate the cliffs. The mule trail is cut into the cliff, and in some places it's not much wider than your mule. You'll clutch your **saddle** when you begin your ride into the canyon. You'll

25 look down 5,000 feet. Your heart will race. But there's nothing to fear. The mules are sure of foot and well trained. You'll soon relax and enjoy the breathtaking scenery. Riders spend the night at the bottom of the canyon at the **rustic** Phantom Ranch lodge. You'll awake to a home-cooked breakfast, with food brought

30 down by mules. Lunch and dinner are also provided.

How and How Much

   Raft trips are offered from April to October. The cost is $565 per person, all meals included. Call *Arizona River Runners* toll-free at 1-800-477-7238 for a free brochure.

35 The overnight mule ride, including all meals and lodging, is $488 for two. There are also day rides part way into the canyon for $85 per person. Reservations are required. For more information, contact: *Grand Canyon National Park Lodges, P.O. Box 699, Grand Canyon, AZ 86023; (602) 638-2401*

*   **swift**
    very fast
    currents
    water flowing in a certain direction
    rapids
    a place in the river where the water moves very fast
    bighorn sheep
    wild, brown Rocky Mountain sheep with big horns
    cacti (pl. of cactus)
    thick plants found in American deserts
    saddle
    a seat for the rider on the back of a mule or horse
    rustic
    very simple or rough

READING 5: *Alone on an Angry Sea*

5–V   With a partner, preview this text. Look at the title, the large type, the photos, and the map/timeline. Discuss what this will be about.

Now read the text as quickly as you can for the main ideas. Don't stop at new words.

> **READING STRATEGY**
>
> Good readers focus on major ideas the first time they read a difficult text.

Tell your partner what you understood.

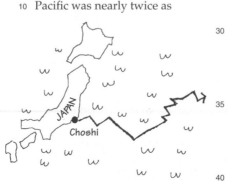

Alone on an Angry Sea

*"*They say that time erases the worst memories. Nothing will erase these.*"*

1   The man was 45 years old. The rowboat was 26 feet long. The ocean was 6,200 miles wide. In July, 1991,
5   Gerard d'Aboville set out to cross the Pacific. He had already rowed across the Atlantic in 72 days. But that was 10 years ago. And the
10   Pacific was nearly twice as wide. Why did he do it? "It's a lot more satisfying than taking the subway," d'Aboville said. Then he added: "It's exciting
15   when you set out to do something that is almost impossible and you succeed. For me, that's happiness." But d'Aboville had no idea of the terror he would
20   experience when he left his wife and two children in Paris to begin the voyage from Choshi, Japan.

D'Aboville's trip from Japan
25   to Washington State lasted more than four months, from July 11 to November 21. Each day he rowed for ten hours. He was in constant danger from
30   strong winds, storms, and even a cyclone. During these storms, he locked himself up in a small cabin, where he felt like he was inside a spinning washing
35   machine. Three times his boat capsized, and once he was tossed overboard and almost drowned. The constant fear of death made it impossible to
40   appreciate the brilliant sunsets

5–W Read the text more carefully. Think about the organization. What information does each paragraph give?

Discuss your ideas with the class.

Frenchman Gerard d'Aboville rowed 8,000 mi. across the stormy Pacific in 134 days.

5–X **Independent Vocabulary Study:** Words for storms and natural disasters. Turn to page 139 in the Vocabulary Appendix.

or the dolphins that played beside the boat. In the end, d'Aboville said, "There were no good moments. When you
45 know that you could die, you don't give a damn about the color of the sky or the sunset…"

When he arrived in Ilwaco,
50 Washington, d'Aboville's back was bent like a bow. A couple of his ribs were fractured. He could barely move his ankles.
55 There was a lack of oxygen in his bloodstream from sleeping in his sealed cabin. He had lost 37 pounds. His wife and children watched him as he sat,
60 small and hunched, not mov-
ing and crying. They didn't know how to react. Should they speak or remain silent. Touch him or not? Then
65 d'Aboville stood up and reached out for an embrace.

From **Life,** *Feb, 1992 (adapted)*

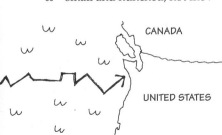

D'Aboville lost 37 pounds during the journey, 29 of them muscle. After sitting for four months, he had lost muscle tone in his back and had difficulty standing straight. But his smile was rejuvenated by two T-bone steaks.

READING 5

5–Y Write your opinion of d'Aboville and his adventure.
Share it with the class.

 5–Z Work in a group of three. Think for a few minutes about a
dangerous or scary experience you have had. Tell your group about it.

Take notes on the stories of your group members.

Story Notes				
Classmates' names	When	Where	Who	What happened

 In your journal or elsewhere, write your story.

READING 6: *Memorable Trips*

We asked two international students: *What was the most memorable trip you've ever taken?* Here are their answers. Which story do you like best?

I love to fish. When I was living in Montreal, two Italian friends and I loaded our car with food and a tent. We drove about 800 kilometers north of Quebec. The road ended at a big lake. We put up our tent and spent a week fishing. I did all the cooking. I'll always remember this trip because I found peace. It was so calm. I really got to know my friends. The solitude made us so close. I loved this trip, and I will see those friends again.

Gianpaolo Conti is from Italy

Quy Thu Nguyen is from Vietnam

When I was 11 years old, I was seldom at home because after school, I went out with my friends everyday. I saw little of my family. My sisters and brothers went to school in the morning and I went in the afternoon. We never met in the day.

One day my parents collected us and said, "We decided you must leave Vietnam. With Communism, you will never have a good future." That night, my sisters, brothers, and I left on a boat. My parents stayed behind because my grandmother didn't want to leave Vietnam.

Before the boat left, my father told us one day we would live together again if God was willing.

We arrived on a small island in Malaysia. I began to cry; now we had to live alone without our parents and manage somehow. At that moment I knew I needed my sisters and brothers for life.

Tell a partner which story you liked best and why.

OPTIONAL READING 7

Sons Help Blind Mom Climb McKinley

THE ASSOCIATED PRESS

1   ANCHORAGE, Alaska—Roped to her twin sons for safety, Joni Phelps inched her way to the top of Mount McKinley, missed her step near a 9,000-foot plunge, then 5 quickly regained her footing.

Phelps, a mountain climber from Pennsylvania, never saw the danger. She has been blind almost half her life.

"They were describing it to me very gen- 10 tly," Phelps, 54, said Friday of the stumble during her climb May 30. "They didn't tell me the worst of it."

The National Park Service says Phelps apparently is the first blind woman to climb 15 the 20,300-foot peak, the tallest in North America.

Phelps' 29-year-old sons moved to Alaska four years ago looking for adventure, but climbing McKinley was their mother's idea.

20   Phelps has relied on a guide dog since she was 30—she began losing her vision in high school. She never gave up her love of the outdoors and has traveled the world, learning to scuba, rock climb and even right a kayak the 25 Eskimo way—by taking a roll in the water.

Phelps worked with a trainer all winter, lifting weights to get strong and learning to tie knots.

"She was prepared, which made us feel 30 confident," Marty Phelps said. He and his brother, Mike, also trained by running, learning to build snow shelters and practicing rescue techniques.

The three spent 16 days climbing 35 McKinley, scaling the mountain in stages to adjust to the altitude.

Joni Phelps, 54, with twin sons Mark, left, and Marty.

On the tenth day, they waited out a four-day storm at 16,000 feet, sitting in their tent behind a wall of snow blocks to keep out high 40 winds.

They continued their climb when the storm ended, and the next day reached the **summit** ridge where Phelps encountered the dangerous ledge known as "Jaws."

45   They spent less than a half-hour at the summit, took a picture and left as the temperature dropped to zero and the wind picked up.

"I knew I couldn't relax after reaching the goal," Phelps said. "I knew we had to get back 50 down."

From **The New Mexican,** *June 7, 1993 (adapted)*

---

* **summit:** top

UNIT REVIEW: *Talk It Over*

Form a group of three or four students. Imagine that you are writing a guide for foreign visitors to the town or city you are living in now. You've decided to put the following page in your guide.

With your group, decide how to complete it.

THE TOP **10**

The best places in _____

Our city has many interesting places to visit, but we especially recommend the following:

Not to be missed ☆☆☆☆

1. _____

2. _____

Highly recommended ☆☆☆

3. _____

4. _____

5. _____

6. _____

Recommended ☆☆

7. _____

8. _____

9. _____

10. _____

UNIT REVIEW: *Writing*

Study the map below. What place are you especially interested in?

Write a letter requesting information about the place. The addresses for the places on the map are on the next page.

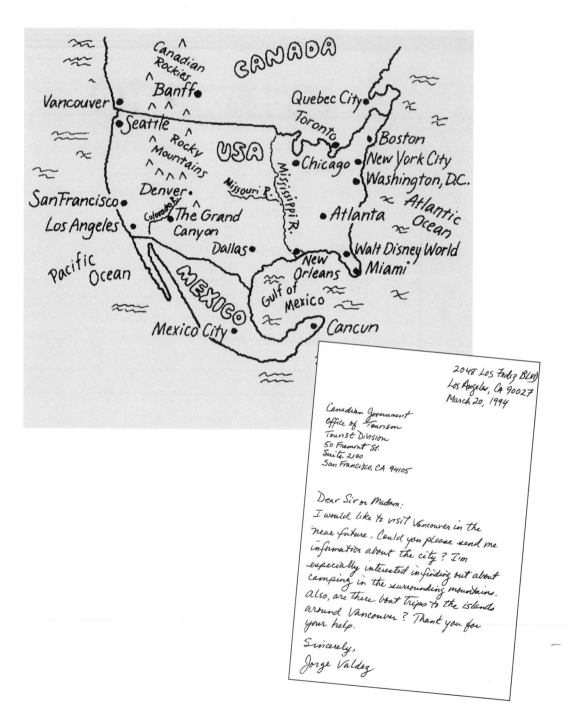

2048 Los Feliz Blvd
Los Angeles, CA 90027
March 20, 1994

Canadian Government
Office of Tourism
Tourist Division
50 Fremont St.
Suite 2100
San Francisco, CA 94105

Dear Sir or Madam:
I would like to visit Vancouver in the near future. Could you please send me information about the city? I'm especially interested in finding out about camping in the surrounding mountains. Also, are there boat trips to the islands around Vancouver? Thank you for your help.

Sincerely,
Jorge Valdez

Atlanta, GEORGIA
Atlanta Chamber of
Commerce
325 International Boulevard
Atlanta, GA 30303

Banff, ALBERTA, CANADA
See CANADA

Boston, MASSACHUSETTS
The Greater Boston Tourist
Bureau
Prudential Tower
Suite 1944
P.O. Box 490
Boston, MA 02199

CANADA
Canadian Government
Office of Tourism
Tourist Division
50 Fremont Street
Suite 2100
San Francisco, CA 94105

Cancun, MEXICO
See MEXICO

Chicago, ILLINOIS
Chicago Convention and
Tourism Bureau
McCormick Place on the
Lake
Chicago, IL 60616

Dallas, TEXAS
Travel Information Services
State Highway Department
P.O. Box 5064
Austin, TX 78763-5064

Denver, COLORADO
Denver Metro Convention
and Visitors' Bureau
225 West Colfax
Denver, CO 80202

Grand Canyon National Park, ARIZONA
Phoenix and Valley of the
Sun Convention and
Visitors' Bureau
505 N. Second Street #300
Phoenix, AZ 85004

Los Angeles, CALIFORNIA
California Office of Tourism
Department of Commerce
1121 L Street
Suite 103
Sacramento, CA 95814

MEXICO
Mexican Government
Tourist Office
10100 Santa Monica Blvd.
Los Angeles, CA 90211

Miami, FLORIDA
Miami Beach Visitor and
Convention Authority
555 175th Street
Miami Beach, FL 33139

New Orleans, LOUISIANA
Louisiana Office of Tourism
P.O. Box 44291
Baton Rouge, LA 70804

New York City, NEW YORK
New York Visitors' Bureau
2 Columbus Circle
New York, NY 10019

Quebec City, QUEBEC, CANADA
See CANADA

San Francisco, CALIFORNIA
San Francisco Visitor
Information Center
Halladie Plaza
900 Market Street
San Francisco, CA 94102

Seattle, WASHINGTON
Washington State
Department of Trade and
Economic Development
101 General Administration
Building
AX-13
Olympia, WA 98504

Toronto, ONTARIO, CANADA
See CANADA

Walt Disney World, Orlando, FLORIDA
Department of Commerce
Visitors' Inquiry
126 Van Buren Street
Tallahassee, FL 32301

Washington, D.C.
Washington Convention and
Visitors' Association
1575 Eye Street NW
Suite 250
Washington, DC 20005

UNIT REVIEW: *Information Tree*

Bring this tree to life! Add some leaves that tell what you remember from this unit.

Arriving in North America

Grand Canyon, Arizona

Alone on an angry sea

Conquering jet lag

A memorable trip

GOING PLACES

 Now compare your tree with a partner's.

UNIT REVIEW: *Word Power*

Group these words and phrases from the unit into the categories below.

~~bus~~	drive	lack of oxygen
row	river	brilliant sunsets
fatigue	ranch	fear
subway	wildflowers	rowboat
fly	dehydration	fractured ribs
canyon	mule	ship
ocean	plane	ride
museum	imbalance	train
jet lag	dolphin	sadness
terror	cliffs	walk
bicycle	airport	stores
cacti		bighorn sheep

Travel			
Forms of Transportation	Ways to Travel (Verbs)	Things to See on Trips	Possible Problems on Trips
bus			

Vocabulary Appendix

1-P DESCRIPTION WORDS

Complete the story about Michael Ho and *feng shui.* Use the descriptive adjectives from below.

✓ Chinese	important	straight
front	lucky	suitable
good	major	unlucky

Michael Ho is a retired professor, and he lives in Covina Palms, California.

Ho believes in *feng shui,* the ____*Chinese*____ word for the "art of placement."

1

For him, a house can be _____ or unlucky.

            2

Professor Ho talked about a house that had several _____.

            3

problems. First, the rear door and the _____ door were in a

            4

_____ line. Second, in the main bedroom there wasn't a

   5

_____ place to put the bed. Ho didn't buy this _____

   6   7

house.

Feng shui tries to create a _____ relationship between people

            8

and the things around them. *Feng shui* is _____ to many Asians, and

            9

to some Westerners, too.

Check your answers on page 140.

1–T MODIFIERS AND NOUNS

In Reading 5, the writer often uses *modifiers* in front of *nouns.* In these examples, which words are the modifiers?

I'm a <u>landscape</u> <u>architect.</u>
<u>Old</u> <u>tires</u> are often given away by <u>tire</u> <u>stores</u>.
Michael Reynolds designs houses out of <u>recycled</u> <u>tires</u> and <u>cans</u>.

Now match a modifier in A with a noun in B. (Note: There is more than one way to match up the words.)

Nouns can be *names* of people, places, things, activities, jobs, and many other things.

Modifiers can be adjectives or other words (including nouns) that give information about a noun.

A	B
aluminum	architect
construction	benefit(s)
environmentalist's	cans
health	dream
interior	material(s)
landscape	store(s)
old	temperature
thick	tire(s)
tire	wall(s)
upper body	work
waste	workout

Now check back on page 14 in the text to see how the writer matched them.

? **Question for Independent Study.** Does your language use *modifier + noun* in the same way as English? Think of an example and tell the class.

1-Z VERBS

Complete the stories using the verbs below. (Each verb needs to agree with its plural or singular subject.)

be (is)	shine	visit
deliver	sleep	wear
live	sniff	look for
take		

A. Many street children sell candy or ___*shine*___ shoes for money. They also
$\underline{\hspace{2cm}}$ drugs for drug traffickers. When these children are hungry, they
2

$\underline{\hspace{2cm}}$ food in trash cans. Sometimes they $\underline{\hspace{2cm}}$ glue. They
3   4

$\underline{\hspace{2cm}}$ dirty clothes. At night they $\underline{\hspace{2cm}}$ on beds of cardboard and
5   6

newspapers. They dream about a normal life.

B. Alexandro is a homeless child. He $\underline{\hspace{2cm}}$ eleven years old, and he
7

$\underline{\hspace{2cm}}$ in the streets of Rio de Janeiro. Sometimes he $\underline{\hspace{2cm}}$ his
8   9

mother; she lives about one hour out of the city. She is poor, so Alexandro

$\underline{\hspace{2cm}}$ her the money he gets from begging or stealing.
10

Check your answers on page 140.

2–T **VOCABULARY REVIEW**

A. Put these words from Reading 6 into the categories below according to meaning.

✓ kill	✓ health	suffer
fatal	longevity	sick
infection	sickness	stroke
disease	headache	outlive
die	pain	murdered
arthritis	suicide	heart attack

LIFE	DEATH	ILLNESS
health	*kill*	

Check your answers on page 140.

WORD FORMS

B. You may have put the following words into the same category. All of them are related to *death*. Fill in these sentences from Reading 6 with the correct word.

death   dead
die   kills
suicide   fatal
✓ murdered

1. Men are ___*murdered*___ more often than women (usually by other men).

2. They commit _____ at a higher rate and have more _____ car

    accidents than women do.

3. Men _____ more often in alcohol-related deaths.

4. Heart disease _____ only one woman (under age 40) for every three men

    in the U.S.

5. But women have an extra decade before their _____ rate from heart

    disease approaches that of men.

6. Men get heart attacks and strokes. Women are sick, but men are _____ .

Check your answers on page 141 or in Reading 6 (pg. 41).

WORD FORMS

C. These word forms are often confused by students. Study them and then fill in the summary below with one of the forms.

die (v)   Men generally *die* younger than women.

died (v, past)   My uncle *died* before my aunt.

dead (adj, n)   My uncle is *dead.*
                       The *dead* should be remembered and honored.

death (adj, n)   The *death* rate from strokes is higher for men.
                       The causes of *death* are different for men and women.

The article "Why Women Live Longer Than Men" explains why men generally ___*die*___ earlier than women. Some of the causes for their earlier
1

_____ are related to the way that men live. They drink and smoke more,
2

and they're more accident-prone. Men's _____ rate is also higher because
3

they don't produce estrogen. This hormone seems to protect women under the

age of 40.

While women don't _____ as early as men, they are sick more often
4

and spend more days in bed than men. As the article points out, "Women are

sick, but men are _____ ." In the past in the U.S., men _____ many
5   6

years before women, but now the gap is shrinking.

Check your answers on page 141.

3–M   WORD FORMS

A. Fill in the blanks with the correct word form. The first sentence in each item comes from "U.S. Families in the 1990s."

1.

> supervise *(verb)*
> supervision *(noun)*
> (un)supervised *(adjective)*

   a) With mother and father both working, children of the Nineties spend more time

     alone and *unsupervised* _____ .

   b) Because they work, parents cannot always _____ their children.

   c) And without proper _____ , many children get into trouble.

2.

> discipline *(verb)*
> discipline *(noun)*
> (un)disciplined *(adjective)*

   a) Child experts such as Dr. Benjamin Spock worry about the disappearance of

     _____ in families where working parents have limited time for their

     children.

   b) When parents don't _____ their children, the children often act in

     very _____ ways.

3.

> satisfy *(verb)*
> satisfaction *(noun)*
> (un)satisfied *(adjective)*

a) The typical mother is working for personal _____ or economic

reasons or, more probably, a combination of the two.

b) Many American women don't feel _____ staying at home all day.

c) Work can _____ their intellectual and emotional needs as well as

their economic ones.

4.

> marry *(verb)*
> marriage *(noun)*
> (un)married *(adjective)*

a) About 60% of all _____ in the U.S. now end in divorce.

b) An increasing number of women who do not _____ are having

children.

c) In 1990, 27% of American children were born to _____ women.

Check your answers on page 141.

VOCABULARY REVIEW

B. Complete the text about families in the U.S. Fill in the blanks with adjectives from the box.

limited	empty	✓ typical
willing	alone	household

In the 1990s, the _____*typical*_____ mother in the U.S. is very likely to be out
1

in the work force. With mother and father both working, American children of

the 1990s are often _____ . Many come home to an _____
2   3

house after school. Child experts worry about the lack of discipline when

working parents have _____ time for their children.
4

Men in the U.S. have new roles in the family. In the 1990s, men are more

_____ to take care of children and cook dinner. These
5

_____ chores are no longer seen as unmasculine.
6

Check your answers on page 141 or in Reading 3 (page 57).

3–X   WORD FORMS

Fill in the blanks with the correct word form. Put verbs in the correct tense.

1.

> marry / get married *(verb)*
> marriage *(noun)*
> married *(adjective)*

Mary Shearing has three children by a previous ____*marriage*____ . She is

_____ to a man 21 years younger. They _____ seven years

ago.

2.

> reproduce *(verb)*
> reproduction *(noun)*
> reproductive *(adjective)*

In the past, women could not

_____ after menopause.

But now, thanks to Martin Luther

Hospital's _____ medicine

program, _____ is

possible for older women like

Mary Shearing.

3.

> fertilize *(verb)*
> fertilization *(noun)*
> fertile *(adjective)*

Because Mary Shearing's eggs were no longer _____ , a younger

woman donated eggs. These eggs were _____ in a test tube, a

procedure known as in-vitro _____ .

4.

> impregnate *(verb)*
> pregnancy *(noun)*
> pregnant *(adjective)*

Mary Shearing wanted to get _____ . But because of her age, her

husband could not _____ her without the help of medical technology.

Her _____ was achieved with the help of Dr. Diaz at Martin Luther

Hospital.

Check your answers on page 141.

4–1 MODIFIERS AND NOUNS

A. In reading 2, you perhaps noticed that many things in the home consist of two words: *modifier + noun.*

Modifier	**Noun**
microwave	oven
videocassette	recorder *(also called a VCR)*

Match the other modifiers with their nouns.

> Nouns can be *names* of people, places, things, activities, jobs, and many other things.
>
> Modifiers can be *adjectives* or other words (including nouns) that give information about a noun.

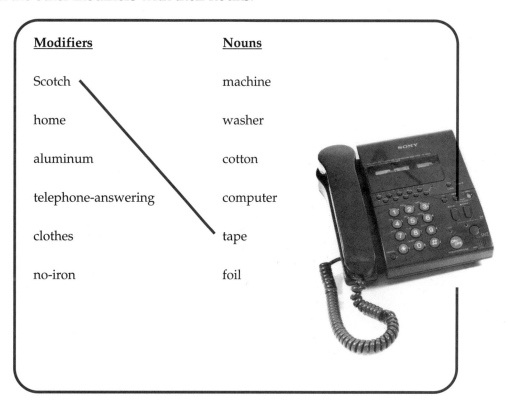

Modifiers	**Nouns**
Scotch	machine
home	washer
aluminum	cotton
telephone-answering	computer
clothes	tape
no-iron	foil

Look back at page 81 to check any phrases you are not sure about.

B. The following are also names of things in the home. Choose the correct modifier for each noun.

1. _____*hair*_____ dryer

2. _____ clock

3. _____ pot

4. _____ telephone

5. _____ mower

6. _____ conditioner

7. _____ opener

8. _____ board

9. _____ cleaner

10. _____ shaker

| cordless |
| hair |
| vacuum |
| can |
| air |
| lawn |
| salt |
| alarm |
| coffee |
| ironing |

Note: Sometimes the two parts (modifier + noun) are written as one word.

lightbulb   armchair

lampshade   dishwasher

Check your answers on page 141.

4–T WORD FORMS

A. These word forms can be confusing. Study them and then fill in the summary below with one of the forms.

choose (v)	When you *choose* a pain reliever, you have to decide between capsules, tablets, or caplets.
chose (v, past)	Yesterday, I *chose* a cereal at the supermarket, but it took me 15 minutes.
choice (n)	Anatoly Rosinsky usually had only one *choice* of beer in Russia.
choice (adj)	I went to the supermarket and found a *choice* piece of meat. (= of excellent quality)
overchoice (n)	For many people, *overchoice* leads to stress.
choosy (adj)	He's *choosy*; he'll only buy the best quality items.

Some experts are wondering if there are too many ___*choices*___ in our
                                                        1
supermarket and department stores. Do we really need more than 40

_____ of cereal? Some people find it stressful to _____ when there
        2   3
are many varieties of an item. They can become emotionally exhausted from a

trip to a shopping mall. But _____ doesn't bother Anatoly Rosinsky, a
                                      4
Russian immigrant. He prefers it to the situation in Russia, where, he claims,

there are too few _____ . Here, with so many varieties, it takes him 30
                          5
minutes to _____ a beer. In Russia, he often stood in line for 30 minutes to
                 6
buy beer. Then, he _____ the one and only beer that was available. In
                          7
such a situation, it is very difficult to be _____ !
                                                    8

Check your answers on page 141.

THE PREFIX *OVER*

B. *Overchoice* means "too much choice." *Over* can be added to the beginning of many words—adjectives, verbs or nouns—to give the meaning of "too much."

What do these words mean?

Adjectives	*Verbs*	*Nouns*
overactive	overspend	oversupply
overweight	overexercise	overexposure
overconfident	overdo	overproduction

Fill in the blanks below with a word beginning with *over.*

1. I _____*overate*_____ yesterday, and I'm not hungry today.
   1
   (I ate too much.)

2. My alarm clock didn't work this morning, and I _____ .
   2
   (I slept too long.)

3. At rush hour, the subways are always _____ .
   3
   (They're too crowded.)

4. The store clerk _____ me for this book.
   4
   (He charged too much money.)

5. I made a lot of money this week because I worked _____ .
   5
   (I worked more time than usual.)

6. Many of our cities are overcrowded and _____ .
   6
   (They're developed too much.)

7. The chef forgot about the meat and _____ it.
   7
   (She cooked it too long.)

8. This test was simple. I _____ for it.
   8
   (I studied too hard.)

Check your answers on page 141.

5–J VERBS INDICATING CHANGE

There are several verbs in Reading 2 that indicate *change*. Look at how they are used.

affect	cause
accelerate	increase
adjust to	

Jet lag usually *affects* travelers going east more than those going west. (affect = produce a change in)

The dry, pressurized air in planes can *cause* dehydration. (cause = make happen)

Don't drink alcohol or coffee, since these liquids *accelerate* dehydration. (accelerate = make happen faster)

Move about the plane. This will *increase* your circulation and help prevent swelling in your ankles and feet. (increase = make or become greater)

Studies show that exposure to strong light can help workers *adjust to* new work schedules. (adjust to = get used to)

Fill in the blanks with one of the verbs above.

1. It's not easy to ___*adjust to*___ life in a new country.

2. Smoking can _____ cancer.

3. Spending a lot of time in the sun can _____ your skin's aging process.

4. Traveling will _____ your knowledge of the world.

5. Jet lag can _____ you for several days after flying.

Check your answers on page 142.

VOCABULARY REVIEW

These words and phrases appeared in Reading 2. Put them into the categories below.

✓ alcohol
imbalance
neckties
jet lag
tight clothes
strong light

✓ liquids
sleep
running suit
swelling
coffee
fatigue

exercise
meat
dehydration
vegetarian foods
ear plugs

Air Travel		
Physical problems associated with it	Things that make you feel better	Things to avoid
	liquids	*alcohol*

Check your answers on page 142.

5–X WORDS FOR STORMS AND NATURAL DISASTERS

cyclone

A violent windstorm moving in a spiral fashion; hurricanes and tornadoes are examples of cyclones.

Match the rest of the words with their definitions.

flood

blizzard

a long period without rain

a shaking of the earth's surface

drought

a large flow of water over dry land

earthquake

a violent snowstorm with strong winds and extreme cold

tidal wave

a large destructive ocean wave caused by an earthquake or cyclone

a storm accompanied by thunder and lightning

thunderstorm

ANSWERS TO VOCABULARY APPENDIX

1–P

1. Chinese
2. lucky
3. major
4. front
5. straight
6. suitable
7. unlucky
8. good
9. important

1–Z

1. shine
2. deliver
3. look for
4. sniff
5. wear
6. sleep
7. is
8. lives
9. visits
10. takes

Unit 1 Crossword Puzzle (page 23)

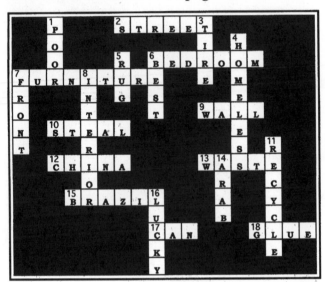

2–T

A.

LIFE	DEATH	ILLNESS
health	kill	suffer
longevity	fatal	sick
outlive	die	infection
	murdered	sickness
	suicide	stroke
		disease
		headache
		pain
		arthritis
		heart attack

B.

1. murdered
2. suicide; fatal
3. die
4. kills
5. death
6. dead

C.

1. die
2. death
3. death
4. die
5. dead
6. died

Unit 2 Crossword Puzzle (page 48)

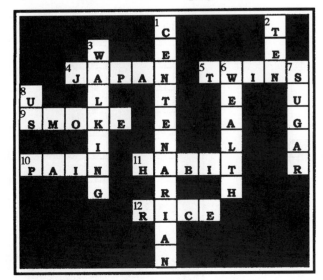

3–M

A.
1. unsupervised; supervise; supervision
2. discipline; discipline; undisciplined
3. satisfaction; satisfied; satisfy
4. marriages; marry; unmarried

B.
1. typical
2. alone
3. empty
4. limited
5. willing
6. household

3–W

1. marriage; married; married/got married
2. reproduce; reproductive; reproduction
3. fertile; fertilized; fertilization
4. pregnant; impregnate; pregnancy

4–I

B.
1. hair dryer
2. alarm clock
3. coffee pot
4. cordless telephone
5. lawn mower
6. air conditioner
7. can opener
8. ironing board
9. vacuum cleaner
10. salt shaker

4–T

A.
1. choices
2. choices
3. choose
4. overchoice
5. choices
6. choose
7. chose
8. choosy

B.
1. overate
2. overslept
3. overcrowded
4. overcharged
5. overtime
6. overdeveloped
7. overcooked
8. overstudied

Unit 4 Crossword Puzzle (page 96)

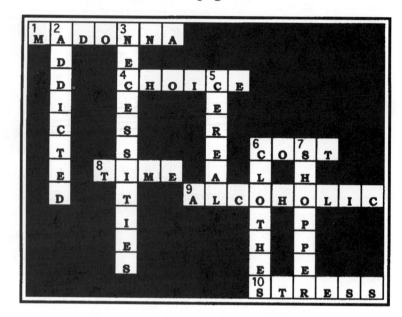

5-J

A.
1. adjust to
2. cause
3. accelerate
4. increase
5. affect

B.

Air Travel		
Physical problems associated with it	Things that make you feel better	Things to avoid
imbalance	*liquids*	*alcohol*
dehydration	*exercise*	*meat*
jet lag	*sleep*	*neckties*
fatigue	*running suit*	*tight clothes*
	vegetarian foods	*coffee*
	ear plugs	
	strong light	

5-X

blizzard	a violent snowstorm with strong winds and extreme cold
drought	a long period without rain
earthquake	a shaking of the earth's surface
tidal wave	a large destructive ocean wave caused by an earthquake or cyclone
thunderstorm	a storm accompanied by thunder and lightning

WORD BANK

Choose words or phrases for your word bank that seem useful to you. These should be words that you might want to use in the near future. You can write on the pages here or use index cards. Make a note first of the **context** in which you found the word. Then use your dictionary to write a **synonym** and a simple **definition.** Write any **word forms** you want to remember.

Look back at your words often. Try to use them in your speech or writing. Try having a partner quiz you on your words.

Sample Entry

Peace (n)	
context:	*"This can mean that money, peace and happiness can escape..." (p. 11)*
Synonym:	*quiet (ness), calm*
Definition:	*freedom from war, noise, or fighting*
Word Forms:	*peaceful (adj)*
	peacefully (adv)

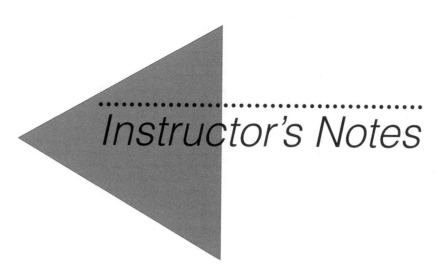

Instructor's Notes

UNIT 1: *Home Sweet Home*

1–A The goal of Activities 1-A through 1-D is to activate students' background knowledge on the unit topic and facilitate entry into the unit's reading texts.

1–B This brainstorming activity can first be done individually. Then students can contribute their ideas to a whole-class brainstorm on the board. (A student volunteer might be willing to take charge of this activity.) You can explore ideas students have about home in the sense of place ("house", "rooms", or "shelter") as well as about people and feelings connected with home ("love", "family", "security").

1–C Have students think about this individually and then share a few of the things they circled, giving reasons.

1–D The purpose of this quiz is twofold: 1) to pique students' interest in the unit readings by showing them they have something to learn, and 2) to give them a quick "tour" of the unit and its specific topics in order to make reading more predictable and hence accessible.

After students finish this activity, they can preview the unit in more depth by paging through it and writing down three things they think they will learn. If you have limited class time, or would like to give students a voice in your curriculum, ask them to choose which readings to cover and which, if any, to omit.

1–F This is a pre-reading activity for the article, "Inside Homes Around the World." Students can describe the house in the picture with a variety of words and phrases. Some of the words and phrases that refer to the picture and which are also mentioned in the following article are:

furniture (type, amount of, arrangement of)

walls and partitions (outside and inside). In the photo, the outside walls are glass.

open floor plan (i.e., absence of walls or doors to separate rooms)

1–G Reading 2, "Inside Homes Around the World," includes an additional pre-reading activity that gets the learner to formulate two useful strategies when first looking at a text. Additionally, the text points out two relevant strategies in the first of the small **Reading Strategy** boxes featured in *Reading Workout:* a) previewing the text, and b) connecting what the reader already knows about a topic with what she or he can learn from a text.

About the Function of the Strategy Boxes and Learner Training:

Reading Strategy boxes are featured throughout *Reading Workout* as a part of learner training. So while the pre-reading and reading tasks are carefully designed to guide the readers to use an appropriate strategy (or strategies) in approaching a particular text, the actual boxes provide both an explicit definition or description of the strategies and a brief rationale for their use in reading generally.

Most recent research in learner strategies supports the use of explicit labels and terms for the strategies learners are using or learning to use. Learner training relies on not only the modeling, but the explicit labeling of strategies.

Previewing (defined in the Reading Strategy box): Readers should get the general idea of a text by looking over the title, subheadings, and the first paragraph. Since this strategy may be new to some students, take time to point out or elicit those parts of the reading that readers can use in previewing.

A second strategy the students are guided to use is that of trying to connect the things they already know with the things they are reading. For this reading, for example, they are asked to put a check next to what they know and a cross next to new information.

1–I This reading activity gets readers to fill in a chart, which in turn can help them comprehend, organize, and recall the information from the text. Students can fill this in as they read (as suggested in the instructions), or after they complete the reading.

1–J Reading 3 offers students a choice of two texts. Encourage students to make an informed choice by previewing the texts. Which one sounds more interesting to them? This functions as a kind of "jigsaw" reading activity.

1–K In this journal writing activity, as in those found in other units in the book, students are given the opportunity to explore their ideas on the general subject area of the unit and react to the readings through personal writing. While several ideas from the previous readings and activities are suggested, students should feel free to write on topics of their choice within the larger subject area.

Why use journals?

An important feature of journal writing in the reading class is that it provides students the opportunity to react to, connect with, and otherwise explore any of the reading topics through meaningful and enjoyable writing. From the instructor's perspective, little work or preparation is required, while valuable insights into the students' attitudes, concerns and points of view can be gained. Students can be encouraged to explore ideas through the use of creative, "groping" language. In the case of journals, instructors can focus their comments on the content and ideas—to what the student is expressing—rather than on aspects of form (grammar, organization, mechanics, and so on). "Quantity" is stressed over "quality."

When, where, how, and how often should students write in journals?

First, you will want to establish whether the students are writing in journals for another class/teacher before you implement this in your reading class. Circumstances such as the number of contact hours, length of class period, goals of the class, and so on, may influence your decisions. You may decide to have students write in their journals either in class, at home, or both. Some instructors prefer to have students write in their journals during the first five to ten minutes of every class, while others give students some class time for this activity one or two times a week. Spending class time discussing the journal topics and options but having students write outside of class is probably optimal. Journals can be collected once or twice a week and returned by the instructor with comments the following day. (Suggestion: For large classes, spread out your reading load by having different journal "due dates" for different groups of students in the class.)

In all cases, allow some flexibility for students who might like to write pages and pages on one topic, as well as for those who prefer to write short entries on several topics. Avoid assigning a specific length or number of words that students must produce. For students who are writing very little, you may want to offer suggestions for expanding and extending what they write. Poems, sketches, maps and any variety of forms can be used in the journals.

What about corrections, responses and other feedback in the journals?

Refrain from making corrections of grammar and form. Focus on the message. If the student has made an error in word choice, comprehension, or idiom—particularly one that may be inappropriate, stigmatizing, or misleading—offer an appropriate alternative word, phrase, or rewording with a short explanation.

Some instructors and students feel that mistakes should not go uncorrected. The research on the effect of instructors' corrections of journals and other written work is far from conclusive. But by focusing on content rather than on form, instructors may be successful in encouraging students to explore their own ideas through freer, more fluent writing. Once students understand some of the rationale behind leaving their journals uncorrected, except for errors mentioned above, they are generally very cooperative.

To react to the content, you will need a

space in which to write. One procedure we recommend is to have students use regular-sized (8 1/2" x 11") notebooks and fold the journal pages or draw a pencil line down the middle of the page. Students write on one side, and you can use the other for your comments. As for peer reading of journals, it is possible to have two- and three-way (or more) reading of journals and responding. To do this, pages can be folded into three columns, allowing for each reader to react and write comments to one another. In our experience, journals have been used more successfully when they are reserved for a personal "dialogue" between student and instructor. Journals should be kept confidential, and a student should be consulted before anything from his or her journal is shared with the class.

1–L This is a pre-reading activity for "Lucky Houses." It activates some ideas about things that are/have good or bad luck in North America as well as in other countries represented in the class. We suggest you take advantage of the cross-cultural differences regarding good and bad luck and superstition as much as possible. Additional good and bad luck symbols are the evil eye (Central Asia, Turkey, North Africa, and parts of the Mediterranean); chile peppers (parts of Latin America and the southwestern United States); spraying water in the path of departing travelers (Croatia and elsewhere); throwing salt over your shoulder, and the number 17 (Italy).

1–M Three important reading strategies are included in 1-M. The first is previewing, already encountered in 1-F. Next, students formulate a question for a classmate as a pre-reading activity that can activate discussion of the upcoming topic. Finally, they are encouraged to form a personal opinion as they read.

1–N   This activity involves a kind of information transfer for students to determine which floor plan conforms to the Chinese criteria for being lucky. After students have had a chance to figure out the "problem," take time to locate the parts of the text that correspond to the lucky or unlucky features of the various plans.

1–O   A feature that appears in all units of *Reading Workout* is a task that has students select their own new vocabulary items from the text to enter into their own **Word Bank** in the back of the book. Or you could encourage the use of 3" x 5" index cards and a file box by each student. Students should be trained to develop and organize their Word Banks according to guidelines that you set. For example, information such as the definition, synonyms and/or the sentence in which the word was encountered can be included. Student-generated vocabulary banks have the advantage of allowing individual students to capture those words that they are ready to put into more active use. Students' Word Banks can also be helpful to you in drawing up vocabulary study lists for the whole class.

1–P   Students can work on this independently, either in class or at home.

1–Q   This is a previewing and pre-reading activity for "Tires Are Hub of New Walls." These activities lead the students through a variation of a classic activity for reading to learn: the SQ3R technique of Survey, Question, Read, Recite, Review. This is a formula for learning from text material, and you may wish to present it to students as a way to deal with academic texts later on when they are reading "on their own." The steps are as follows:

1. Survey (preview) the text to discover its general outline and main point(s).

2. Ask yourself questions about the text and topic.

3. Read the text.

4. Recite by giving answers to the questions raised in step 2.

5. Review the material.

1–S   You or a student can also write the information from the chart at the board or at the overhead projector.

The pair activity under 1-S encourages personal reactions to the very alternative home described in Reading 5. When discussion winds down, you can elicit some of the reasons why different students would or would not like to live in the Degan-Siegel home, and list them in two columns at the board.

1–T   Students can work on this independently, either in class or at home.

1–U   This functions as a pre-reading task for "Brazil's Children of the Streets."

1–W   This summary chart gives main information in the form of answers to six questions: who, what, where, why, when, and how many? Although summarizing is a type of skill most students will know about, it remains one of the most difficult yet crucial reading and writing tasks in academic contexts. Activity 1-W further clarifies what a summary is for the students. The rationale for summarizing is also given in the Reading Strategy box. After the students fill in all the information, you might want them to read or write it out as a summary paragraph.

1–X   For a discussion of uses of journals, see 1-K.

1–Y   The first sample summary has at least 3 problems:

1. It contains opinions (e.g., "I like Alexandro" and "We should help him."
2. It has changed the facts ("… because he has no parents." In fact, Alexandro has parents, and they are poor.)
3. It includes details, such as the fact that Alexandro has curly hair.

The second summary meets the requirements for a good summary.

The third summary has one main problem: It is copied extensively from the original. Additionally, it doesn't mention *why* Alexandro (or any of the other millions of children) live on the streets—a key point in the text.

Optional Reading 7

This is an extra text for students who are motivated to read on their own. You may, however, choose to use it in class with a small group reader response activity as a follow-up.

Unit Review: Talk It Over

This activity uses the widely known "Find someone who …" technique, which gets students to circulate and ask one another questions. If the class is large, instruct students to write a different name in each blank. If it's small, eliminate this restriction. Tell students to let you know immediately when they have filled in all the blanks. The "winner" should be allowed to tell the class whom he/she has found for each item.

Unit Review: Writing

Expect that student interest may vary a lot in this writing activity. Encourage as much creativity as possible in the style and format of poems. You can point out that words from their Word Bank will be a source of good words to include.

UNIT 2: *To Your Health*

2–A The goal of Activities 2-A through 2-D is to activate students' background knowledge on the unit topic and facilitate entry into the unit's reading texts.

2–B This brainstorming activity can first be done individually. Then students can contribute their ideas to a whole-class brainstorm on the board. (A student volunteer might be willing to take charge of this activity.) After a number of words and phrases are on the board under the two categories, ask students to study the categories to see if they agree with the placement of the items. There may be disagreement on some items such as "sun," which can be healthy in moderation but not in excess, or "fish," which, when containing mercury, can be unhealthy. Encourage discussion.

2–C Have students think about this individually and then share a few of the things they circled, giving reasons.

2–D The purpose of this quiz is twofold: 1) to pique students' interest in the unit readings by showing them they have something to learn, and 2) to give them a quick "tour" of the unit and its specific topics in order to make reading more predictable and hence accessible.

After students finish this activity, you might have them preview the unit in more depth by paging through it and writing down three things they think they will learn. If you have limited class time, or would like to give students a voice in your curriculum, ask them to choose which readings to cover and which, if any, to omit.

2–F This is a pre-reading activity for the article, "Bad Habits That Can Ruin Your

Health." As students write, circulate to help them express their ideas.

2–G To further illustrate "scanning," ask students to tell how they read a menu. Do they read it from start to finish? Or do they look at the headings (*Appetizers, Salads, Drinks, Desserts,* etc.) first to see which parts of the menu they want to read? Most readers would not read this text from start to finish, but rather would read selectively, and this task attempts to reflect this real-life reading situation.

Try giving students a time limit of five minutes or so to read about their bad habits. Then pair students off to have them tell each other what they learned. This can function as a kind of "jigsaw" reading activity.

2–I To develop strategies for faster reading and better comprehension, students need, as much as possible, to be weaned from an over-dependence on their dictionaries. Stopping too often to look up new words not only slows second-language readers down, but it can also interfere with comprehension. Students need to develop an awareness, firstly, that not all words in a text carry the same amount of meaning; unknown words peripheral to the central idea of a text can, in many cases, be ignored. Secondly, students need to develop confidence in guessing at the meaning of unknown words when the context is rich enough. To give students additional help with the concept of guessing from context, put the following sentences on the board and have them guess the meanings of the underlined words and tell how they guessed.

- I didn't eat breakfast or lunch today and I'm *ravenous*. Let's go to dinner soon.
- The *clutter* in Molly's apartment was unbelievable. There wasn't even an empty chair to sit on.

2–K This is a pre-reading activity for "In Eating Habits, East Is Better Than West." It is aimed at getting students thinking about their own eating habits prior to reading about the diets of Americans and Chinese.

2–L If you have students from China or Japan in your class, they might like to comment on this article after all students have finished reading and answering the question at the bottom of the page. Do they agree with the assertions the article makes about the diet in their countries?

2–N The first portion of this activity functions as a comprehension/review exercise for Reading 4. Students will need your guidance for the dictation portion below.

2–O Students can add words in these boxes, too, if they remember any (such as those on page 33).

2–P If you have students from Japan in your class, let them comment on this article. Perhaps they are familiar with Kin and Gin, can explain why they are so popular, or can provide other information about Japan's stars. Their classmates may want to ask them some related questions as well. This text and accompanying exercises to some extent set the stage for Reading 6.

2–Q Give students a minute or two to think individually or in pairs about possible reasons. A student volunteer could then go to the board to record the class' predictions. The activity would work well as a group task also.

2–S This activity functions as a comprehension task and also focuses students' attention on the medical vocabulary of the text. Students could check their charts with a partner or with you.

2–T   Students can work on this independently, either in class or at home.

Optional Reading 7

This is an extra text for students who are motivated to read on their own. You may, however, choose to use it in class with a small group reader response activity as a follow-up.

Unit Review: Talk It Over

(P. 46) For a discussion of uses of journals, see 1–K.

(P. 47) If your class is large, instruct students to write a different name in each blank. If it's small, eliminate this restriction. Tell students to let you know immediately when they have filled in all the blanks. The "winner" should be allowed to tell the class whom he/she has found for each item. If students don't know each other well, have them raise their hands as the "winner" mentions them.

UNIT 3: *Family Ties*

3–A   The goal of Activities 3-A through 3-D is to activate students' background knowledge on the unit topic and facilitate entry into the unit's reading texts.

3–B   This brainstorming activity can first be done individually. Then students can contribute their ideas to a whole-class brainstorm on the board. (A student volunteer might be willing to take charge of this activity.) Encourage discussion.

3–C   Have students think about this individually and then share a few of the things they circled, giving reasons.

3–D   The purpose of this quiz is twofold: 1) to pique students' interest in the unit readings by showing them they have something to learn, and 2) to give them a quick "tour" of the unit and its specific topics in order to make reading more predictable and hence accessible.

After students finish this activity, you might have them preview the unit in more depth by paging through it and writing down three things they think they will learn. If you have limited class time, or would like to give students a voice in your curriculum, ask them to choose which readings to cover and which, if any, to omit.

3–F   For item 1, students may know statistics about divorce in their countries and the U.S. Their answer for this would then be based on fact rather than opinion.

3–G   Encourage students in groups to give reasons for their opinions. Are they basing their opinions on personal observations, things they've read, things they've seen on TV, or things they've heard about? In the process, students should share a lot of information about family structures and roles of family members in their countries.

3–H   Reading 2 offers students a choice of two texts. Encourage students to make an informed choice by previewing the texts. Which one sounds more interesting to them? This functions as a kind of "jigsaw" reading activity.

3–J   This is a pre-reading activity for "U.S. Families in the 1990s." This could be done as a whole-class activity on the board, with either you or a student volunteer writing down predictions.

3–K   The purpose of this activity is to have students experiment with attacking a tough text in a global way for the first reading. The strategy of going first for general ideas in a text and getting details in a second reading is often more efficient than reading a text just once in a careful and labored way.

3–L This chart can be gone over in any way that makes sense: in pairs, groups, or with the whole class.

3–M Students can work on this independently, either in class or at home.

3–N This activity calls for students to integrate material from the text they have just read as well as from their personal experiences of family life in both the U.S. and their countries. Manipulating textual data in this way hones the academic skill of actively linking what one reads with what one knows.

3–O For a discussion on the uses of journals, see 1–K.

3–P This activity functions as a pre-reading activity for "Male Couch Potatoes" and attempts to get students thinking about roles of men and women in the home.

3–Q This is a preview activity for "Male Couch Potatoes." Remind students that previewing a text allows them to make certain predictions about its content before reading and is a strategy good readers use.

3–R **3–S** You may wish to further expand here on the uses of the reading strategies *scanning* and *skimming*. Students should be aware that the way a reader approaches a given text will depend upon the reader's purpose and what that reader wants from a given text. When we *scan* a text, our eyes jump around the text in a non-sequential order to find specific information. Readers usually scan bus or train schedules; they often scan menus, directories, and the like. Longer texts such as the one in question may be scanned when a specific piece of

information is needed. When a reader wants to get the gist of a text, he/she *skims* it. When skimming, a reader's eyes move sequentially and quickly over a text.

3–T This reader response activity encourages students to see texts as something with which they can engage. In addition, it hones critical thinking skills.

3–V This is a previewing and pre-reading activity for "Grandma Conceives Twins At Age of 53." Together with the following activity, it leads students through a variation of a classic activity for reading to learn—the SQ3R technique of Survey, Question, Read, Recite, Review. This is a formula for learning from text material, and you may wish to present it to students as a way to deal with academic texts later on when they are reading "on their own." The steps are as follows:

1. Survey (preview) the text to discover its general outline and main point(s).
2. Ask yourself questions about the text and topic.
3. Read the text.
4. Recite by giving answers to the questions raised in step 2.
5. Review the material.

You may prefer to have students write their questions individually or in pairs rather than as a whole-class activity on the board.

3–W This reader response activity encourages students to see texts as something with which they can engage; in addition, it hones critical thinking skills.

3–X Students can work on this independently, either in class or at home.

3–Y The purpose of this activity is to get students to compare two related texts. They have quite a bit of background knowledge going into this text, as readers often do, and this activity will, it is hoped, sensitize them to the fact that the knowledge one brings to a text plays an important role in reading.

Optional Reading 7

This is an extra text for students who are motivated to read on their own. You may, however, choose to use it in class with a small group reader response activity as a follow-up.

UNIT 4: *Born to Shop*

4–A The goal of Activities 4-A through 4-D is to activate students' background knowledge on the unit topic and facilitate entry into the unit's reading texts.

4–B This brainstorming activity can first be done individually. Then students can contribute their ideas to a whole-class brainstorm on the board. (A student volunteer might be willing to take charge of this activity.) Encourage discussion.

4–C Have students think about this individually and then share a few of the things they circled, giving reasons.

4–D The purpose of this quiz is twofold: 1) to pique students' interest in the unit readings by showing them they have something to learn, and 2) to give them a quick "tour" of the unit and its specific topics in order to make reading more predictable and hence accessible.

After students finish this activity, you might have them preview the unit in more depth by paging through it and writing down three things they think they will learn. If you have limited class time, or would like

to give students a voice in your curriculum, ask them to choose which readings to cover and which, if any, to omit.

4–F This is a pre-reading activity for the article, "Favorite Things, Timesavers All." Before reading about what Americans consider "necessities," students are asked to consider the question themselves.

4–H This article has some complex structures and vocabulary. Point this out to students and tell them they need not understand everything to get the main ideas.

4–I Students can work on this independently, either in class or at home.

4–J This is a pre-reading activity for "Compulsive Shopping Viewed as Addiction." Help students understand the headline prior to their reading.

4–K This reader response activity encourages students to see texts as something with which they can engage; in addition, it hones critical thinking skills.

Encouraging students to discuss their impressions and reaction to a text, rather than answering teacher or textbook-produced questions, will give students more responsibility for their own reading and more control over their own learning.

4–M This is a pre-reading activity for "Madonna and Money." Give students a few minutes to make their estimates and then have them share information in pairs, groups, or with the whole class.

4–N This reader response activity encourages students to see texts as something with which they can engage. In addition, it hones critical thinking skills.

This might be a good opportunity to

discuss some differences between academic expectations in North American colleges and those of students' countries. Analyzing, expressing opinions, and thinking critically about texts may not be as valued in students' countries. The memorization and replication of factual information in texts may be more highly valued.

4–P This is a pre-reading activity for "Overchoice."

4–R In discussing the category that the writer falls in, you may wish to bring up the phrase *point of view*. Writers bring a point of view to material they write. A good reader needs to discover that point of view and evaluate the evidence to see where she or he stands.

4–S This is another activity focused on getting students to guess at meaning from context. If your students don't have adequate oral skills to do this in English, consider suggesting that groups can discuss in their native languages.

See 2-I in these Instructor's Notes for a rationale of why an activity like this can help develop useful strategies for second-language readers.

4–T Students can work on this independently, either in class or at home.

4–U This discussion activity aims to get students thinking about "overchoice" in a broad sense. In general, do they feel bombarded by too much choice in areas of their lives? Or do they feel their options are too limited in certain areas? Cross-cultural comparisons might also be interesting in this context.

4–V Reading 6 offers students a choice of two texts. Encourage students to make an informed choice by previewing the texts. Which one sounds more interesting to them? This functions as a kind of "jigsaw" reading activity.

Optional Reading 7

This is an extra text for students who are motivated to read on their own. You may, however, choose to use it in class with a small group reader response activity as a follow-up.

Unit Review: Talk It Over

If your class is large, instruct students to write a different name in each blank. If it's small, eliminate this restriction. Tell students to let you know immediately when they have filled in all the blanks. The "winner" should be allowed to tell the class whom he/she has found for each item.

Unit Review: Writing

For a discussion of the uses of journals, see 1–K.

UNIT 5: *Going Places*

5–A The goal of Activities 5-A through 5-D is to activate students' background knowledge on the unit topic and facilitate entry into the unit's reading texts.

5–B This brainstorming activity can first be done individually. Then students can contribute their ideas to a whole-class brainstorm on the board. (A student volunteer might be willing to take charge of this activity.) Encourage discussion.

5–C Have students think about this individually and then share a few of the things they circled, giving reasons.

5–D The purpose of this quiz is twofold: 1) to pique students' interest in the unit readings by showing them they have something to learn, and 2) to give them a quick "tour" of the unit and its specific topics in order to make reading more predictable and hence accessible.

After students finish this activity, you might have them preview the unit in more depth by paging through it and writing down three things they think they will learn. If you have limited class time, or would like to give students a voice in your curriculum, ask them to choose which readings to cover and which, if any, to omit.

5–F This is a pre-reading activity for "Conquering Jet Lag." To survey the class, simply ask for a show of hands for the first two questions. For the third question, ask students, *Has anyone taken a really long plane trip?* Ask those who raise their hands to tell how long their flights were. Ask the person taking the longest trip the last question. Students, meanwhile, can take notes on the entire interaction.

5–G After groups have had a few minutes to preview the article and talk about its organization, ask for their conclusions and see if the groups agree. Some may include the introductory portion of the text in their count of "major parts," while others may not.

5–H After students read and extract the information that is new to them, they are instructed to tell a partner what they've learned. The "How You Read" box focuses students' attention on the importance of talking about what one reads. Talking about reading is a helpful tool for most readers because it allows reformulation of textual material. This reformulation facilitates content learning. You might point out to students that when they begin their regular academic studies, forming study groups to discuss readings will help them learn.

5–I The first portion of this activity functions as a comprehension/consolidation/review exercise for Reading 2, "Conquering Jet Lag." Students will need your guidance for the peer dictation task. Try modeling the task with a student prior to having pairs begin.

5–J Students can work on this independently, either in class or at home.

5–K This activity functions as a pre-reading activity for the two texts in Reading 3. Both are accounts of first days spent in the U.S.

5–L Make sure that students understand that they have a choice of two texts to read here. Give students five minutes or so to read the text they've chosen.

5–M Help students pair up with one or two partners who read a text they did not read. This is a type of "jigsaw" reading, which forces students to try to summarize for each other what they read in order to achieve a goal—in this case, the goal of finding similarities in the stories.

5–O Ask students to circulate around the class and talk to five classmates about their "first day" experiences in North America. If you are in an EFL setting outside of North America, you will want to skip this activity.

5–P For a discussion of the uses of journals, see 1–K.

5–Q   As students talk, give the class time to take notes on what their classmates say. This task will get them to focus more carefully on their classmates' comments.

5–R   This brainstorming task functions as a pre-reading activity for "Grand Canyon, Arizona." This could also be done as a whole-class activity, with a student volunteer writing on the board.

5–S   This text has a very clear-cut organization marked by subheadings, so students should have little difficulty grasping the main ideas by previewing.

5–T   This is another activity focused on getting students to guess at meaning from context. If your students don't have adequate oral skills to do this in English, consider suggesting that groups can discuss in their native languages.

See 2-I in these Instructor's Notes for a rationale of why an activity like this can help develop useful strategies for second-language readers.

5–V   The purpose of this activity is to have students experiment with attacking a tough text in a global way for the first reading (*skimming*). The strategy of going first for general ideas in a text and getting details in a second reading is often more efficient than reading a text just once in a careful and labored way.

5–W   The three paragraphs in this text lay out the following information: 1) a general introduction to d'Aboville and his trip; 2) actual details about the experience of crossing the Pacific; and 3) information about d'Aboville and his family after the trip. You might incorporate a general discussion about the purpose of paragraphing into this activity.

5–X   Students can work on this independently, either in class or at home.

5–Y   This reader response activity encourages students to see texts as something with which they can engage. In addition, it hones critical thinking skills.

5–Z   Give students both a thinking period and a time limit for this activity. You might give students a few examples of scary experiences you have had to get them thinking. Students who can think of no scary experiences might be able to tell about a scary dream they have had or a scary experience of a family member.

Optional Reading 7

This is an extra text for students who are motivated to read on their own. You may, however, choose to use it in class with a small group reader response activity as a follow-up.

Unit Review: Talk It Over

After groups have completed this task, you may want to do one of the following things so that all groups can read each other's work: 1) have each group transfer its recommendations onto poster board and tack them up on the wall; 2) make photocopies of each group's work to give to the other groups; or 3) if you have a large blackboard, have each group write its results there.

INDEX

Photo Credits:

Jann Huizenga: pp. 1, 8, 9, 44a, 49, 54, 55, 63, 87, 92, 94, 113a; Kim Crowley: pp. 25, 30, [appendix 11, appendix 12]; Laura Husar, The New American: 4; A/P World Wide Photo: pp. 8, 64, 65, 68, 69, [appendix 10]; Ezra Stoller/ESTO: p. 5; Kyodo News Service: p. 38; Nancy Hunter Warren: p. 40; Mia Thomas Ružić: pp. 44b, 44c, 113b; Robert Brenner/PhotoEdit: p. 52; James Higgins/Higgins & Ross: p. 69; Ranko Ružić: p. 75, 97; UPI/Bettmann: p. 85; People Weekly © 1993 Mimi Cotter: p. 90; George Kanatous: p. 91; Egyptian Tourist Authority: p. 98; FPG International: pp. 102, [appendix 16]; Atlanta Ballet: p. 104; Grand Canyon Nat'l Park Lodges: p. 108; T.J. Conroy/Terra Photo: p. 109; Dominique Hubert/SYGMA: p. 110, 111; Anchorage Daily News/Fran Durner: p. 114.

Reading Credits
(adaptions and reprints):

"Lucky Houses," p. 11: Condensed with permission from the *Atlantic Monthly.* "Tires are the Hub of New Walls," p. 14: *The New Mexican,* 1992. "Brazil's Children of the Street," p. 17: Copyright © Associated Press, reprinted with permission. "A Day in the Homeless Life," p. 19: adapted with permission from the Associated Press. "Bad Habits that Ruin Your Health," p. 30: © 1987, Meredith Corp., all rights reserved, reprinted from *Ladies Home Journal* with permission of the author. "Two for the Ages," p. 38: People Weekly © Time Inc. "Why Women Live Longer that Men," p. 41: Condensed from an article by Edward Dolnick in *Health* (July/August 1991), © 1991. "Are You Cancer–Prone?" p. 43: Reproduced from *Health Risks,* by Elliott J. Howard, M.D., and Susan A. Roth, published by Body Press, a division of HP Brooks, Inc., a division of Price Stern Sloan, Inc., Copyright © 1986 by Elliott J.

Howard, M.D., and Susan A. Roth. "Male Couch Potatoes," p. 60: © Associated Press, reprinted with permission. "Grandma Conceives Twins at Age of 53," p. 65: Copyright © by Associated Press, reprinted with permission. "Grandma, 53, Delivers Twins," p. 68: Copyright © Associated Press, reprinted with permission. "Favorite Things," p. 81: Copyright © The New Times Company, reprinted with permission. "Compulsive Shopping Viewed as Addiction," p. 82: Copyright © Associated Press, reprinted with permission. "Overchoice": p. 87. Reprinted with permission, Los Angeles Times Syndicate. "A Change of Heart," p. 90: People Weekly © 1993. "Helping Others," p. 91: Excerpted with permission from *What It's Like to Win the Lottery* by Per Ola and Emily d'Aulaire, Copyright © 1986 The Reader's Digest Assn., Inc. Maniya Barredo's oral history: p. 104: "Honey," from *New Americans: An Oral History* by Al Santoli, Copyright © by Al Santoli, used with permission from Viking Penguin, a division of Penguin Books, USA, Inc. "Here I Am a Stranger," p. 105: from *Two Years in the Melting Pot* by Liu Zongren. Reprinted with permission from China Books. "Alone on an Angry Sea," p. 110: Copyright © Sygma, Adapted with permission. "Sons Help Blind Mom Climb Mt. McKinley," p. 114, Copyright © Associated Press, reprinted with permission.

Sally Forth Cartoon: p. 61, reprinted with special permission of North American Syndicate.